Hamlyn All Colour

INDIAN
COOKBOOK

Hamlyn All Colour

INDIAN
COOKBOOK

Zuju Shareef · Tim Luxton

HAMLYN
London · New York · Sydney · Toronto

Contents

Cover and inside photography by Bob Komar
Authors' photographs by Peter Maynard
Illustrations by Ann Rees

Published in 1984 by
The Hamlyn Publishing Group Limited
London · New York · Sydney · Toronto
Astronaut House, Feltham, Middlesex, England

ISBN 0 600 32436 2

Set in Monophoto Apollo
by Photocomp Ltd, Birmingham, England
Printed in Italy

Useful facts and figures

Notes on metrication

In this book quantities are given in metric and Imperial measures. Exact conversion from Imperial to metric measures does not usually give very convenient working quantities and so the metric measures have been rounded off into units of 25 grams. The table below shows the recommended equivalents.

Ounces	Approx g to nearest whole figure	Recommended conversion to nearest unit of 25
1	28	25
2	57	50
3	85	75
4	113	100
5	142	150
6	170	175
7	198	200
8	227	225
9	255	250
10	283	275
11	312	300
12	340	350
13	368	375
14	396	400
15	425	425
16 (1 lb)	454	450
17	482	475
18	510	500
19	539	550
20 ($1\frac{1}{4}$ lb)	567	575

Note: When converting quantities over 20 oz first add the appropriate figures in the centre column, then adjust to the nearest unit of 25. As a general guide, 1 kg (1000 g) equals 2.2 lb or about 2 lb 3 oz. This method of conversion gives good results in nearly all cases, although in certain pastry and cake recipes a more accurate conversion is necessary to produce a balanced recipe.

Liquid measures The millilitre has been used in this book and the following table gives a few examples.

Imperial	Approx ml to nearest whole figure	Recommended ml
$\frac{1}{4}$ pint	142	150 ml
$\frac{1}{2}$ pint	283	300 ml
$\frac{3}{4}$ pint	425	450 ml
1 pint	567	600 ml
$1\frac{1}{2}$ pints	851	900 ml
$1\frac{3}{4}$ pints	992	1000 ml (1 litre)

Spoon measures All spoon measures given in this book are level unless otherwise stated.

Can sizes At present, cans are marked with the exact (usually to the nearest whole number) metric equivalent of the Imperial weight of the contents, so we have followed this practice when giving can sizes.

Oven temperatures

The table below gives recommended equivalents.

	°C	°F	Gas Mark
Very cool	110	225	$\frac{1}{4}$
	120	250	$\frac{1}{2}$
Cool	140	275	1
	150	300	2
Moderate	160	325	3
	180	350	4
Moderately hot	190	375	5
	200	400	6
Hot	220	425	7
	230	450	8
Very hot	240	475	9

Notes for American and Australian users

In America the 8-fl oz measuring cup is used. In Australia metric measures are now used in conjunction with the standard 250-ml measuring cup. The Imperial pint, used in Britain and Australia, is 20 fl oz, while the American pint is 16 fl oz. It is important to remember that the Australian tablespoon differs from both the British and American tablespoons; the table below gives a comparison. The British standard tablespoon, which has been used throughout this book, holds 17.7 ml, the American 14.2 ml, and the Australian 20 ml. A teaspoon holds approximately 5 ml in all three countries.

British	American	Australian
1 teaspoon	1 teaspoon	1 teaspoon
1 tablespoon	1 tablespoon	1 tablespoon
2 tablespoons	3 tablespoons	2 tablespoons
$3\frac{1}{2}$ tablespoons	4 tablespoons	3 tablespoons
4 tablespoons	5 tablespoons	$3\frac{1}{2}$ tablespoons

An Imperial/American guide to solid and liquid measures

Solid measures	
IMPERIAL	AMERICAN
1 lb butter or margarine	2 cups
1 lb flour	4 cups
1 lb granulated or caster sugar	2 cups
1 lb icing sugar	3 cups
8 oz rice	1 cup

Liquid measures	
IMPERIAL	AMERICAN
$\frac{1}{4}$ pint liquid	$\frac{2}{3}$ cup liquid
$\frac{1}{2}$ pint	$1\frac{1}{4}$ cups
$\frac{3}{4}$ pint	2 cups
1 pint	$2\frac{1}{2}$ cups
$1\frac{1}{2}$ pints	$3\frac{3}{4}$ cups
2 pints	5 cups ($2\frac{1}{2}$ pints)

Note: When making any of the recipes in this book, only follow one set of measures as they are not interchangeable.

Introduction

Co-authorship means co-approval. I approve of Zuju and she approves of me. If she doesn't she's far too diplomatic to say so. We met in Iran. Zuju was hunting through the bazaars for new herbs and spices, rediscovering the land of her grandmother. I was a shipping agent. An unlikely starting point for a cookbook, you might say, but we're both Sagittarians and capable of anything. Zuju is completely Indian while I'm ill at ease in my British skin. Together we make a brilliant team.

Our friendship couldn't fail to flourish once I'd tasted Zuju's food – I'd never eaten anything like it. Up until then my experience of Indian cooking was characterised by a positive response to spicy food. But Zuju took pity on me and staged a series of cookery classes in a bid to show me what real Indian food was all about. About ten of us squeezed into her kitchen and watched as she demonstrated the subtle art of grinding saffron or, and this is by far the most important thing we learnt, how to treat basmati rice as a living thing.

Zuju was so relaxed and confident during the lessons that we encouraged her to write a book. The discussions about it span three years and half the world. At first in the sweltering heat of Khorramshahr, Iran (before the revolution), then in the Rue des Plantes, Paris 14eme and finally up and down the length of Britain, including London W8 and of course Pond Cottage, Zuju's home.

About a year after we'd escaped the revolution, I asked Zuju how she was getting on with the book.

'Very slow,' she said, 'but why don't you help me, Tim? Fifty, fifty.' With more Indian food in the offing, I could hardly refuse and without a second thought I agreed. Shortly afterwards I disappeared to France and that put the book back another year. However, when it was eventually finished, God was merciful to us – he brought Eleanor in to help. Eleanor Lines is an old friend of mine and a real gem. It's thanks to her generosity of spirit and active support that the book is in your hands today.

There's one more thing to say. Throughout the writing of this book, we were both frequently attended by another Sagittarian, Zuju's daughter, Juhi. While we spent our time struggling with measurements and ingredients, Juhi battled with her homework. At the time she was six. Her English homework had the flavour of one long recipe, while characters in her essays kept talking about the meal they'd had the night before. Juhi will never turn into a glutton, she spends more time talking about the food than eating it. But she'll definitely be a good cook. Indian cooking, Zuju's Hyderabadi way, is no more difficult than Juhi's first recipe, written at the grand old age of six and a half.

'Take a chikan put it in a pot with sum salt add garlik and it is dun.'

It really is as simple as that.

Spices and ingredients

Spices are the foundations of Indian cookery; every dish incorporates a pinch of something, if only chillies. Indian cuisine is impossible in the absence of spices. The cook who has already tried his or her hand at 'curries' of one sort or another may think, quite rightly, that there's nothing new here. If you can already distinguish poppy seeds from mustard seeds, or cumin from kalonji, then consider this section as a refresher course and at least check up on the spices you don't know. If on the other hand you have often been hopelessly confused by endless lists of spices, in quantities which often seem geared to industrial manufacture, then read on. Some dishes genuinely need a wide selection of spices, but many can be cooked using five or six spices which are easily available. Indians don't use curry powder; they use individual spices, varying the choice and quantity for each and every dish. Occasionally a selection of spices are ground together: garam masala is the obvious example, but this is prepared separately for each dish.

In this chapter the spices are grouped according to their functions which not only include flavouring but also thickening. So that you will be as familiar with the use of a pinch of chilli powder as you are with a pinch of salt, the spices are explained as follows:

1 The Standard Four
2 Hara Masala
3 Curry Leaves (*Kariapath*)
4 Garam Masala
5 Pickling Spices (*Achar Ke Masala*)
6 Spices and Essences for Desserts

THE STANDARD FOUR

This is a collection of four basic spices – chillies, turmeric, ginger and garlic – which are regularly used in the recipes throughout this book. A number of excellent dishes can be prepared using just these four spices. The Standard Four are almost always used together but occasionally one or other of them may be excluded from a particular dish; for example, ginger is used only sparingly with fish because it can make the flesh disintegrate.

Chillies (*Mirchi*) and **Chilli Powder**   Chillies are an essential ingredient and they are found in every Indian kitchen. Some other spices may be overlooked if need be, but without chilli powder you won't be able to make a start.

Grown on bushes, chillies vary in size and are at first green, but as they ripen they turn red. They are picked while green for immediate use, or they are laid out to dry in the sun. When well dried they turn scarlet and are used either whole or they can be ground down to make chilli powder. *It is in the powder form that chillies are most commonly used in the Standard Four.*

When fresh, chillies have the texture of a green pepper and they vary considerably in strength. They are used chopped, sliced, crushed or slit lengthways. Once slit, the chillies are opened out and the seeds scraped out with the blunt edge of a knife. This is a laborious process, but worthwhile because the seeds tend to give a bitter – and hot – flavour to the cooked dish. When the chillies are cooked whole the stalks are left intact as they are supposed to absorb any bitter taste which the chillies may give.

The 'hotness' of Indian food is directly attributed to the quantity of chillies used in the preparation. Tastes vary from household to household, some people like their food hot, others less so. Although chillies make the food hot, if used in moderation they do not conceal or spoil the other flavours.

Washed and dried, chillies keep well in the vegetable compartment of the refrigerator.

Turmeric (*Haldi*)   Turmeric is a bright yellow root. It is boiled, then ground to a powdered form. Sold in tins or packets, turmeric is readily available in supermarkets. It has no particular flavour, and in some Eastern countries it is referred to as *zard choob* or yellow wood. However, it has strong preservative qualities and it is essential in most pickles. Traditionally it is also used in paste form to counteract itches and skin diseases, and also as a depilatory!

Turmeric colours food as well as drawing out and balancing other flavours. It has the undesirable effect of turning green vegetables a greyish colour, so avoid using turmeric when cooking spinach and other greens. These vegetables can also acquire a bitter flavour from turmeric.

Ginger (*Adrak*)   This is a swollen root or rhizome. It can be frozen; alternatively it keeps quite well in a cool place or it will keep even better placed in a small pot and covered with sandy soil. Fresh ginger should have the firmness of a potato, if it is allowed to dry out it tends to become wrinkled, shrunken and woody.

The skin is peeled or scraped off the fresh ginger using a knife or potato peeler. The ginger can then be blended in a liquidiser with a drop of water to make a paste, or used either thinly sliced or finely chopped. If you want a dish to offer sudden bursts of ginger flavour, then use it sliced. Used as a paste, or finely chopped, its flavour will be evenly distributed. Beans, lentils and peas are almost certainly cooked with ginger because it also helps to counteract flatulence.

Garlic (*Lehsun*)   Garlic is widely used in Indian cookery, although traditionally its benefit to the flavour of a dish was questioned. Used chopped or sliced, in whole cloves or ground (like ginger), garlic can also be mixed with a little water to make a fine paste. In the form of a paste it keeps well for a fortnight in an airtight container in the refrigerator. Garlic and ginger complement each other and they are often used together. Ginger controls the tendency which garlic has to overpower other flavours and it also seems to reduce its lingering persistence on the breath.

There are no particular proportions in which to use the Standard Four it is much better to discover what suits you best. However, to avoid disastrous first encounters, try using these spices in the following proportions: 1 teaspoon ground garlic (or 2 large cloves, crushed) to $\frac{3}{4}$ teaspoon ground (or grated) fresh root ginger, $\frac{1}{2}$ teaspoon chilli powder and $\frac{1}{4}$ teaspoon turmeric. You can adapt these proportions, adding more ginger, less chilli or another clove of garlic, just as you please.

HARA MASALA

Hara Masala is a mixture of two fresh herbs – coriander leaves (cothmir) and mint (pudina) – and fresh chillies. Chopped finely and mixed together, these ingredients are used primarily as a garnish; occasionally they are incorporated with a dish.

Coriander Leaves (*Cothmir*)   Fresh coriander is used in all middle eastern cookery. It can be bought from Greek, Turkish and Indian grocers, as well as some supermarkets and greengrocers.

Coriander leaves resemble a plain, large-leaf variety of parsley, but only in appearance. There is no similarity in the flavour and parsley cannot be used as a substitute for coriander.

When young and tender, both leaves and stalks are used but only the leaves are used from an older plant. Unfortunately chopped coriander does not keep for long and it soon wilts. Bunches of coriander can be wrapped in muslin and stored in a plastic bag in the vegetable compartment of the refrigerator.

Alternatively, if there's no supplier nearby, it can be chopped and frozen.

Most commonly used as a garnish, coriander can also be used in the *dum-dena* technique and it is often used in chutneys. Dried coriander leaves can be used after soaking them in water, but the flavour will not be as good.

Mint (*Pudina*) There are far more varieties of mint available in Europe than in India. Use common mint, or whichever type is available. The leaves are used whole, chopped or ground to a paste. Mint has a strong flavour and it is used more sparingly than coriander. A few stalks of mint will keep for some time in a jar of water, then you can break off the leaves as required.

Fresh Chillies (*Mirchi*) In hara masala fresh chillies are chopped, and the patient cook removes all the seeds because they are very hot. As with coriander or mint, chillies are used either to flavour foods during the *dum-dena* technique, or they are ground to a paste in chutneys. They are also combined with coriander and mint for garnishing dishes.

Once you get used to eating hot food you'll probably find yourself using more and more chillies. However, an ability to eat hot food has nothing to do with an appreciation of Indian cuisine; it's simply a question of habit.

Here is a rough guide to the proportions to use in the preparation of hara masala; once again decide what combination suits you best. Use 3 teaspoons chopped coriander to ½ teaspoon chopped mint and 2 or 3 chillies.

CURRY LEAVES
(*Kariapath*)

Curry leaves look similar to bay leaves, but they are thinner and not as wide. These leaves are used fresh and they are essential for Hyderabadi cookery. Without curry leaves, Khatti Dal, the staple Hyderabadi lentil dish, is somewhat bland. Curry leaves are also used in liquid dishes in the company of souring agents – a combination which tends to bring out the full flavour of the food.

Commonly used throughout south India but not in the north, curry leaves are not as easily available in Britain as other spices. However, it is definitely worth making a bit of an effort to obtain the leaves. Buy plenty when you find them, then rinse and dry the leaves and wrap them, five or six at a time, in cooking foil. Each packet will be enough for one dish and these can be kept in the freezer for up to ten months.

If you cannot get the fresh variety, then use the dried leaves. Once soaked in a little water, the dried leaves are an excellent second best.

GARAM MASALA

Although chillies are hot to the taste, they are in fact considered to be cooling because they promote perspiration and this cools the body. In contrast the garam masala spices have more flavour, are not as hot as chillies and have the effect of warming the body. In the tropical south the food is much hotter than it is in the north, where winters mean snow and Kashmir shawls, and garam masala takes precedence over chillies.

Garam masala is the term used to describe one spice, or a combination of spices, which are mixed together before use; but it is not a curry powder. Garam masalas can vary from dish to dish, and using the spices ready mixed from a tin will not give the required result. The following spices are used in the preparation of garam masala: black pepper (*kala mirchi*), cloves (*long*), cardamoms (*illyachi*), cinnamon (*dar chini*), black cumin (*shah zeera*) and kabaab spice (*kabaab chini*). These spices are

garlic

ginger

mint

coriander

fenugreek

curry leaves

fresh chillies

chilli powder

turmeric

used either whole or in powdered form, depending on what's cooking. They all keep well in airtight containers.

Black Pepper (*Kali Mirchi*)   Next to chillies, this is the spice most commonly used throughout India. The peppercorns are used whole, crushed or ground. In south India they are used when they are green for cooking and also for pickling; they are also recommended for relieving digestive ailments.

Cloves (*Long*)   Cloves have a powerful aroma and flavour. If too many are used, the other flavours in the dish are well and truly lost because the cloves march firmly to the front line. However, when used with care they enhance a number of dishes, especially desserts.

Cardamoms (*Illyachi*)   These are the dried seed pods of a palm. There are three varieties: green, white and black. Inside the pod, it is the tiny black or beige seeds which contain the flavour. The seeds pods are used whole or ground; they have a strong sweet flavour and are considered to be something of a luxury due to their expense. The white and green varieties are used in both savoury and sweet cooking, while the black ones are only used for savoury food. Children are given a seed to chew as a treat and adults chew them after meals to refresh the breath. It's quite common to have a small plate of these and also betel nuts (*chikni*) to pass round after a meal.

Cinnamon (*Dar Chini*)   Well known to all, this is the aromatic inner bark of the cinnamon tree. Small pieces of the bark are used whole or they can be ground into a fine powder. Cinnamon is easily obtainable, both in the form of sticks and ground.

Black Cumin (*Shah Zeera*)   This seed is dark in colour and occasionally called *siah zeera* or *kala zeera*. Not to be confused with the common white cumin which is easily available, black cumin has a very subtle flavour which is easily drowned if too many of the other garam masala spices are used. Rice (excluding the 'par-boiled easy to cook' variety which is sold everywhere) has a delicate fragrance of its own which can be easily masked when combined with a strong spice; but when rice is cooked with black cumin the subtle flavours of both can be fully appreciated. A well-stocked delicatessen or Indian grocer should have black cumin but it is not an essential ingredient. So if you cannot get hold of it don't worry – you'll still be able to cook good food without it.

Kabaab Spice (*Kabaab Chini*)   This spice is typical of Hyderabadi cuisine and it's so named because of its importance in making kabaabs. Kabaab spice is usually used to replace cloves and black pepper and these can be used instead of it, but the flavour is not quite the same. Kabaab spice is another extra, so don't worry if you can't find it anywhere.

A combination of the garam masala spices, used in the following proportions, can be ground and kept ready for use: 2 teaspoons black cumin seeds, 1 teaspoon ground black pepper, 8 green or white cardamoms (discard the outer pods and use only the seeds), 5-cm/2-in piece cinnamon stick and 8 cloves. Although this mixture is an excellent standby, it will not fulfil the requirements of every recipe, so you may find alternative suggestions as you read through the book.

PICKLING SPICES
(*Achar Ke Masala*)

This is a collection of five spices which have a less specific function than any in the first three groups. They are coriander (*dhania*), cumin (*zeera*), mustard seeds (*rai*), onion seeds (*kalonji*) and fenugreek (*methi*), and they are used in *baghars*, or to complement the garam masala, or some of them may occasionally be used with the Standard Four Spices; they are also invaluable for pickling. Coriander and cumin are both used a great deal in the south of India, while cumin is more popular in the north.

Coriander (*Dhania*)   Coriander seeds should grow well in the garden. Plant a few seeds and you will have the double benefit of fresh coriander throughout the summer months, then a supply of new seeds at the end of the season. When dried, these seeds turn pale beige in colour. They are commonly used in Indian cooking for thickening gravies and they give a fresh lively zest to vegetables and dried beans.

The plant and seeds differ slightly in flavour; and the seeds are often roasted before they are used either crushed or ground. If they are insufficiently ground the seeds may be fibrous but a little more grinding will turn them into a fine powder. Often the whole seeds are used, or they may be used coarsely crushed, alternatively finely ground coriander is used in some khormas and pickles.

Cumin (*Zeera*)   These are thin long seeds which are beige in colour and they can be used whole, ground or roasted to achieve different results. Cumin has a strong flavour and a smell which dominates the Indian spice markets. It is quite often added to Hyderabadi *baghars*, or used in some karis and yogurt preparations.

Mustard Seeds (*Rai*)   Although you are probably accustomed to using mustard in its prepared form, the seeds may not be as familiar. They are tiny tan coloured or cream droplets with a smooth matt texture. In India one mustard seed is sewn into a child's cap to give protection from evil spirits. In cooking, both the cream and dark varieties are commonly used either whole or ground for *baghars* or for pickling. Mustard seeds have a very sharp taste which is easily misjudged, so be careful not to overdo it when adding the seeds to your cooking.

Onion Seeds (*Kalonji*)   Onion seeds are small black, slightly twisted seeds. They are used very sparingly, either whole or ground and mostly for pickling.

Fenugreek (*Methi*)   Fenugreek is the most powerful of all the spices. The small flat mustard-coloured seeds (which resemble tiny pebbles) are used whole or ground. The whole seeds are used in *baghars* and the ground seeds are used in pickles. Like coriander, the plant is also used as a herb (but not in hara masala) and the flavours of both plant and seeds are quite distinct with a tendency to linger.

SPICES AND ESSENCES FOR DESSERTS

Sweet in India means very sweet indeed. Nobody can, or for that matter should, eat a great deal of any Indian dessert. These sweets are made with a mixture of ingredients which frequently include milk, ground nuts, eggs, fruit and carrots. Fresh carrots are quite sweet and for this reason they are used more often in desserts than in savoury dishes. The desserts always use a lot of sugar, whether pure and white or raw, and each dessert is flavoured with any of the following spices: saffron, cloves, cardamoms, nutmeg and mace. Cloves and cardamoms have already been discussed as part of garam masala. Saffron must take pride of place over all the spices used in sweet cooking, but in addition there are the essences (*ittars*).

The two most commonly used essence ingredients are keora (also known as *screw-pine* and *gullab*) and roses. These are diluted with water to make keora water and rose water which are both available from Indian grocers. There are also many other essences, for example, *khas* is a variety of grass used to make fans and grass curtains (which freshen the air) and it is also used in desserts. *Shamama* is a herbal essence often used at weddings and it is thought by some to be an aphrodisiac. There are the flowers – *motia*, *sada bahaar* and *chambelli* (jasmine) – and, of course, sandalwood and musk. The essences of all these are diluted with water and a few drops are added to flavour sweets.

Saffron   Saffron is made from the dried stigmas of the saffron flower, a plant which is similar to a crocus and which is specially cultivated in Kashmir. It is understandably the most expensive spice in the world, because a pound of saffron requires the patient collection of the stigmas from at least seventy thousand flowers. It comes in strands or in a powdered form, but it is best to buy the strands, as the powder may not be pure. Although it's expensive, the strong sweet smell of saffron means that only a few strands are needed for any dish. It's expense naturally tends to restrict its use to special rice dishes and, of course, desserts.

Cloves (*Long*)   The fact that cloves have a strong flavour has already been mentioned – this is just a reminder. However, this potency can be used to advantage but you will still only need two or three cloves in a dish to serve four to six people.

Cardamoms (*Illyachi*)   Only the green and white cardamoms are used in desserts and the large dark brown ones, which have a mellow nuttier flavour, are reserved for use in meat dishes. The cardamom pods can be used whole or sometimes the tiny black seeds are removed and ground.

Mace (*Juz*) and **Nutmeg** (*Javatri*)   Mace and nutmeg both come from the nutmeg tree which is native to the Moluccas (a group of islands in Indonesia). The ripe fruit splits to expose the dark brown nut, or nutmeg, which is surrounded by a bright red membrane – the mace. The mace is stored until it dries to a yellowish orange, then it is cut into fine slivers ready for use. Although they come from the same plant, mace and nutmeg do not have the same flavour and they are not interchangeable.

Keora   Keora essence is extracted from the inner leaves and the flower petals of a small palm common to south India. Not only is it used in desserts but it is also found in some meat and rice dishes.

Rose Water (*Gullab*)   Rose essence is extracted from specially cultivated dark pink roses. Because of its popularity, the rose essence is used as a base for rose water, rose-flavoured syrup and preserves. Rose water is also used to flavour drinks.

Silver Foil (*Varak*)   This is a very thin edible silver foil made from fine silver film. It is available in small sheets from Indian grocers and it is used to decorate desserts, kabaabs and some rice dishes. There is so little silver in one sheet that *varak* is not too expensive.

Nuts and Seeds

The use of oily nuts and seeds is common throughout India, especially in Hyderabad and in the north where, for example, the use of almonds and pistachios to thicken sauces adds a rich and subtle smoothness.

Coconut (*Copra*)   Coconuts provide the mainstay of life to the coastal populations of south India. The coconut trees are used in boat building, the branches are utilized for making huts, the leaves are used for weaving mats and thatching, and the coconut itself provides more still. The coconut fibre is used to make ropes and, before even getting to the flesh, the liquid inside the coconut (which is not the milk) makes a refreshing drink. The white coconut flesh is used in cooking and, when grated and pulped, it yields a creamy milk which plays an equally important part in some dishes. In addition, oil is extracted from the fruit.

   Fresh coconut has more flavour than the desiccated variety, but it does require lengthy preparation. Coconut is sometimes roasted before cooking and it is used in both sweet and savoury dishes.

Peanuts (*Moom Phalli*)   Peanuts are used either raw or roasted, but they are not used frequently.

Almonds (*Badaam*)   In India almonds are used in both sweet and savoury dishes. Don't buy ready ground almonds if you can avoid it, because they tend to lose their flavour. Buy the shelled

mace

nutmeg

cinnamon sticks

coconut

peanuts

almonds

pistachio nuts

chirongi

cardamoms (white and green)

cardamoms (brown)

nuts, blanch them and remove their skins, then soak them before use. They can be used trimmed into thin slivers or ground down to a powder.

Pistachios *(Pistas)* Pistachio nuts are widely available in their shelled or unshelled form. The shells crack easily, exposing a spring green nut with outer tints of violet. They are used mainly in desserts and, like almonds, they can be blanched, chopped or ground. Although pistachios are expensive they repay every penny of their cost with their excellent flavour.

Poppy Seeds *(Khash Khash)* These are tiny ivory or beige coloured seeds. They are used either roasted to a dark brown or in their natural state and they add their own unique flavour to any dish.

Sesame *(Til)* Used in savoury dishes, and generally roasted before use, sesame seeds are flat, slightly oval and cream coloured. They are about the same size as mustard seeds.

Chirongi These are also known as *chirolo* or *charooli* but they have no English name. The small, pale, slightly flattened seeds or nuts are mottled with dark patches. They are commonly used in kabaabs, khormas and some desserts. You will only be able to buy chirongi from a well-stocked Indian spice merchant or grocer.

ONIONS

Onions play a fundamental role in all Indian cookery. Occasionally they are used as the main food in a recipe, but more often they are a basic ingredient to bring out and complement the flavours of the spcies and also to thicken sauces and gravies. Cooked onions are slightly sweet in flavour and it is this sweetness which tends to neutralise and complement the sourness and occasional pungency of some of the spices.

Most commonly the onions are sliced or chopped, then fried in a little oil as the starting point of any number of dishes. However, at different times and for different reasons, they are also used raw, roasted, fried and grilled. Their taste varies not only according to how they are cooked but also depending on the way they are cut. Quartered and cooked as a main vegetable they take on a taste of their own. Onions are regularly used in chutneys and, blended in the liquidiser, they are the principal ingredient and thickening agent in the gravies for koftas and khormas. They are also cooked with kabaabs to keep them moist and tender. As a fresh garnish with coriander and mint, onions are very finely sliced, washed, then separated into rings. To add zest, the onion rings can be mixed with a little lemon or lime juice.

SOURING AGENTS

In the southern areas of India most meals are served with a sour pickle or at least one dish prepared with a souring agent. This is not true of the North; in Gujarat for example all main meals are accompanied by a sweet dish.

There are a number of seasonal bitter fruits that are used to add the sour flavour which is essential in Hyderabadi cooking. Most of these fruits are also made into pickles, while the sweet fruits that grow in south India are used mainly for desserts and only occasionally in chutneys. Although the following fruits are not available in Britain they may give you some idea of what the south Indian markets offer. *Be Lumboo* is the same shape as a gherkin but it has the texture of a gooseberry. *Halfa leori* is an extremely sour pale yellow berry with a hard seed (or stone) similar to a cherry. Another berry, *karondeh*, is green flecked with purple, and *narangi* is a cross between an orange and a lemon. All these fruits are in season at different times of the year and when available they make a change to the diet.

Apart from these unusual ingredients, green tomatoes, malt vinegar, yogurt, lemons, limes, mangoes and tamarinds are all used as souring agents. There should be no trouble in obtaining all these, though you will probably have to go to an Indian grocer for tamarind. With the exception of yogurt all the souring agents have a triple function: they can be used as marinades, as a medium to mix the spices or they are used for their flavour and texture.

Yogurt *(Dahi)* Yogurt can be used in chutneys or raitas, as the thickening ingredient for a sauce, or as a marinade for kabaabs. Then, of course, it's also used for sweets, or served on its own as a mild accompaniment to hot curries. Whether you buy it or make your own yogurt, make sure you always have some in the refrigerator. Yogurt is popular throughout south India, it is extremely versatile and will be in constant demand for the recipes throughout this book.

Tamarind *(Imli)* Tamarind and yogurt are the most commonly used souring agents. Tamarind comes from the runner bean shaped fleshy pod of the tamarind tree which is native to India. Fresh tamarind can occasionally be found in Britain – the pod should be peeled, the seeds removed and the flesh or pulp compacted into cakes. The dried brown cakes of tamarind are available in Indian grocers and they keep for a long time.

To make tamarind extract wash and soak the cake of dried tamarind in warm water. About a handful of tamarind and half a cup of water will be enough for a dish to serve four to six people. Once the water has been soaked up, the cake gets soft and mushy. Use your fingers to mix it into a pulp then press this through a sieve. The stalk, husk and coarser parts of the pod are left behind and the fine pulp and juice collected. Another half cup of warm water may be used to wash through any goodness that remains in the husk.

If all this seems a little tedious, you'll be pleased to know that the pulp can also be obtained in its extracted form. This is a concentrated pulp and it must be diluted before use. To obtain the right consistency, dilute 2 teaspoons of the concentrate with 300 ml/$\frac{1}{2}$ pint water. When tamarind extract is listed in a recipe, this is the liquid which is required.

Mango The smaller the mango the more sour it is. An unripe mango has a soft seed which hardens gradually as the fruit ripens. When the seed is hard, but the mango is still green, this is the best time to use the fruit for making pickles and chutneys. Often, in India, mangoes are used in a dried form as mango powder or *amchoor*. Mangoes are peeled before use, then the smallest ones (about 4 cm/$1\frac{1}{2}$ in long) are used whole, while the flesh of the larger ones (up to 15 cm/6 in) is cut into strips before use.

PAPAYA

Papaya, or paw-paw as it is sometimes named, is a large fruit grown on palm trees native to Asia and Africa. A small piece of the raw fruit is ground into a purée and this is spread on meat or mixed with mince to act as a tenderiser. Indian meat is lean but to make it tender everyone uses papaya; it's quite natural and essential to achieve the correct consistency for kabaabs. However if papaya is not available a commercially prepared meat tenderiser can be substituted.

LENTILS AND PULSES

Lentils and pulses are nutritious and versatile, and they provide a regular supply of protein in all aspects of Indian cookery. Here are some of their uses: they are ground and used to make certain types of bread, mixed with water and used as a batter, mixed with meat as a binding ingredient for kabaabs or ground, mixed with spices, soaked and used to make fritters. A mixture of one or more lentils and pulses are often cooked with rice, alternatively they can be soaked, dried and fried as a light crunchy snack. Boiled they are the major ingredient of a number of dals and karis, or they can be added to meat and vegetable dishes. Occasionally the lentils can be used to thicken sauces or sprouted for use in salads.

Despite modern packaging, most lentils have a certain amount of dust or even a few small stones mixed with them. To clean the lentils a very simple method called *dholna* is used and this is not unlike panning for gold. The lentils are washed and rinsed in a sieve, then placed in a bowl and topped up with water. The lentils are slowly rotated in this bowl, then the top layer (together with some of the water) is transferred to a second bowl. By the time all the lentils have been transferred to the second bowl in this way most of the grit will have sunk to the bottom of the first bowl. The process is continued until the lentils are completely clean.

Alternatively the lentils can be spread on a plate and those which are inedible can be picked out. Both methods are equally effective, but the former method will enable you to handle more lentils after a little practice.

Red Lentils (*Masoor Dal*)   The whole lentils are dark green in colour and may even be black. Once the skin is removed and the lentils are split the dal turn out to be the familiar red lentil commonly available in most shops. This is used in both dry and liquid dals. The whole green lentil can be cooked with rice.

Split Black Beans (*Maash ki Dal, Urud or Urd Dal*)   When whole, this dal is black; however, the skinned split version (which is considered a delicacy) is white with a subtle flavour.

Soak the dal for 2 hours before cooking so as to improve the final texture. During cooking a froth will form on the surface of the water and this should be skimmed off. There will also be a strong, not altogether pleasant smell but this will disappear when the lentils are cooked.

Gram Lentils (*Channa Dal*)   Raw channa dal are called 'boot' in Hyderabad. These are green lentils, grown on bushes in small pods containing two or three lentils. They are in season in early winter and, despite the work involved in collecting enough for one dish, they are most popular. The dried lentils are brown and, when split, resemble split peas in colour and shape. The split channa is used in dals, vegetable dishes or boiled with a few herbs and spices. In kabaabs and some koftas the ground dal is used to help bind the minced meat. Also ground, the channa dal makes a pale yellow flour known as *besan*. Apart from cooking, this flour is mixed to a paste for use as a face pack or, in the form of a thin paste, it is used as a shampoo. Tamarind and fenugreek are also used as hair preparations.

Chick Peas (*Chole*)   Most people know what chick peas look like. In India chick peas are subservient to lentils but they are still extremely popular. To get the best from chick peas, soak them for at least 3 to 4 hours. They are usually boiled but occasionally they are used in slow-cooked dishes or stews. Soaked, then quickly fried they make a delightful snack.

Mung Beans (*Mung ki Dal*)   When whole these are small round olive green beans; when split and skinned they are yellow. They cook quite easily but again it is best to soak them for at least an hour. After this, 30 to 40 minutes boiling will be enough and they will be sweet and tender. After overnight soaking the beans can be blended with a little water and spoonfuls of this batter can be deep fried to make *bhajjias*.

In the west, mung beans are frequently associated with bean sprouts. Although the Chinese may have introduced these, sprouted pulses are also commonly eaten throughout India.

To sprout all lentils and pulses, first remove the stones and grit and carefully wash the beans. Put them in a dish with just enough water to cover them and leave the dish in a warm place. The airing cupboard is the most obvious place or they can be left next to a radiator. Top up with fresh water morning and night for 2 to 3 days by which time the mung beans should have sprouted. The shoots should be about 0.5–1 cm/$\frac{1}{4}$–$\frac{1}{2}$ in long and at this stage they have the best flavour. The larger the sprouts grow the more their taste is dissipated. Different lentils take different times to sprout and this time depends on their size or the warmth of the growing place. Once sprouted, the beans should be washed again and they can then be served with a vinaigrette dressing, on their own or with other vegetables.

dried limes

qhoobani

tamarind

red lentils (whole and split)

black beans (split and whole)

gram lentils (whole and split)

chick peas

toovar dal

mung beans (split and whole)

Cooking techniques

The success of Indian cooking depends on three basic factors: the choice of spices, the quantity of spices used and the way in which the flavour of the spices is introduced into the food. There are three techniques which are used to combine the flavour of the spices with the other ingredients and these are used separately or combined at different stages of the preparation of any particular dish. These techniques have the effect of coaxing the full subtlety and flavour of each spice into the food. Each spice has a personality of its own and when treated with consideration this will flourish, but if the spices are disrespected they can turn nasty. Cumin, for example, when misused will often overpower the food with a strong murky flavour; you will taste nothing but the bitterness of the cumin and the dish will be a black or earthy brown colour.

This section is intended to help you to acquire a grasp of the cooking techniques and methods of preserving the personalities of the spices. The three basic techniques are *bhun-na*, *baghar* and *dum-dena*. These techniques are straightforward and simple but there is never enough emphasis laid on their importance.

BHUN-NA

Fresh herbs and spices give up their flavour almost immediately. There is little comparison between fresh herbs and their dried counterparts. Packets of dried herbs and spices often look quite miserable but their flavour is lying dormant. Consider them in hibernation; what they need is a good shake up to arouse their individual personalities and get them to work. This is what *bhun-na* is all about. In the absence of this technique the resulting dish will have a somewhat raw aroma and flavour. There are two methods of doing this – roasting or frying.

Bhun-na Roast   Roasting is the simpler of the two methods. In India the spices are roasted very quickly on a hot griddle (called a *tawa*) which can be quite satisfactorily replaced by a saucepan. Use a saucepan with a lid because some seeds (such as poppy seed or sesame seeds) get more shaken up than others and they are liable to pop and jump all over the kitchen.

Put the saucepan on the cooker and heat it up. When it's quite hot, put the seeds in, cover with the lid, and keep shaking the pan until the spices are roasted evenly. Shaking the pan prevents any of the spices from burning. The *bhun-na roast* has been carried out correctly when all the individual seeds have turned a rich golden colour. Don't overdo it, or leave the spices

in the saucepan once the right colour has been achieved, or else they may burn. A heavy-based saucepan is quite liable to take the cooking beyond the point of no return and you will end up with little grains of charcoal. The smaller the nuts or seeds, the quicker they will roast but you do not have to roast each type individually. Start with the largest ones, then (as they are roasted) progressively add the remaining seeds and nuts finishing with the smallest. For example, first roast coriander seeds, then add cumin seeds and finally add poppy seeds which only take a few seconds to roast. Experimentation is the best guideline here.

The *bhun-na roast* not only awakens the spices but it drives off their moisture and ensures that pickles (and some dishes that are kept for a few days) do not go off.

Bhun-na Fry   This is usually carried out at the beginning of cooking but occasionally it may take place at the end or even in the middle of a recipe. The spices can be fried separately or together with other ingredients like onions, poultry or vegetables; the more the spices are fried the darker the result. Remember, the *bhun-na* process, whether roasting or frying, represents one part of the overall cooking of the dish, so the spices will not be completely cooked at this stage. It's best to fry the spices just long enough for the raw smell to disappear, by which stage their flavour will be fully awakened, then follow on with the other stages and the final technique of *dum-dena*.

Oil is heated in a pan, then the spices are added with the onions or sometimes the onions are cooked first. When the spices are dry and ground, a little water is added so that they do not burn or turn brown too quickly. Freshly ground spices, such as ginger or garlic, contain a little water so it is unlikely that you will have to add any extra liquid. With a little practice you will know when to add extra water. Once the spices have been added to the oil, keep stirring them to ensure even frying. If you're not careful the spices tend to stick to the base of the saucepan and once this happens they can quickly burn. If, despite your close attention with the spatula or wooden spoon, the spices still insist on sticking, add a little water.

When *bhun-na frying* at the end or during the cooking processes, take care not to stir too vigorously or otherwise the meat or vegetables are liable to break up. The water content has to be reduced considerably before the frying can take place; if there's too much liquid you'll be stirring a stew.

BHAGHAR

If you've ever tried to make dal and it turned out like lentil soup, there's one simple explanation – you forgot to do the *baghar*. With this technique tucked firmly up your sleeve, friends will think you've spent years in India studying the culinary arts.

Oil is heated in a small frying pan or saucepan. Indian cooking requires the use of a lot of oil in some dishes and the thick layer of oil on top of the food is all important for the flavour. Once the oil is hot, add the whole spices (or onions, herbs or a mixture of all these) and fry them until they are golden brown. The secret of *baghar* is that the entire contents of your pan (oil and spices combined) are now poured, hissing, on to other cooked or partially cooked ingredients – for example, meat, vegetables or pulses. As soon as the contents of the pan have been emptied on to the other ingredients, jam a lid on the dish or pan so that the aroma and flavour stays in.

The *baghar* is usually carried out at the end of cooking, but occasionally it's carried out right at the start. Be careful not to overfry the spices and *don't add any water*. If you have to add other ground spices to the oil, first let the hot spices cool slightly, then when you add the additional spices there should be no trouble. The smell of this cooking process is quite powerful and the mixture of oil and spices distinctly changes the flavour of the dish with which it is being used. Most pickles are made using this process. The ingredients most commonly used for *baghar* are onions, garlic, whole mustard seeds, cumin, dried lentils, chillies, curry leaves, fenugreek, onion seeds and rice. These are not used together, but depending on the dish, one, two or more will be chosen.

DUM-DENA

This is an essential aspect of Indian cookery. Just as the *bhun-na* gave the spices a jolt into wakefulness and the *baghar* keeps a dish on its toes, *dum-dena* gives the food a chance to catch its breath and relax. In Iran this is called *dum bekushe*, which literally means 'to draw breath'. In India, where cooking takes place over wood fires, *dum-dena* is carried out in a vessel which is specially adapted for the job. The pear-shaped pot containing the food is placed on a cool bed of charcoals, then the top of the pot is covered by a concave lid which is also filled with slow burning charcoals. *Dum-dena* may take from five minutes to two hours for perfect results. You probably don't have a charcoal fire so, once cooked, the food can be placed in a very low oven. Alternatively, the pan can be left, tightly covered, on top of the cooker over a very low heat.

During *dum-dena* two important processes take place; first the oil used during cooking rises to the surface, giving the dish a finished appearance, and secondly the flavour of the spices completely penetrates the meat or vegetables. *Dum-dena* is the secret of cooking rice so that each grain ends up separate and fluffy.

black peppercorns

cloves

cumin seeds
(white and black)

saffron strands

mustard seeds

sesame seeds

fenugreek seeds

coriander seeds

poppy seeds

onion seeds
(kalonji)

Fish and seafood

"So sorry, it's against my religion" was the favourite let out clause used by an Iranian photographer from Abadan whenever he didn't want to do something. He used the remark almost indiscriminately; his religion was highly personalised and effortlessly flexible.

Eating fish other than scaly fish is against Zuju's religion. This belief is obviously based on local Hyderabadi traditions. At monsoon time, a large round freshwater fish called *murral* appears in the market. This is a family favourite and it is frequently cut in steaks and cooked with a selection of spices.

In Britain, Zuju's religion becomes a little more flexible; here she uses cod, haddock and halibut. The fish recipes in this chapter also include prawns. In Hyderabad fish is always bought live, but there's no chance of buying live fish in Britain, so when you buy fish make sure the eyes are not cloudy – the clearer the eyes, the fresher the fish.

Fom the left: Hot Tempered Prawns (page 28), Seasoned Fried Fish (page 25) and Fenugreek Fish (overleaf)

Fish Stuffed with Fresh Herbs

Hari Bhari Machi

1 (1.5-kg/3-lb) salmon trout, cleaned
oil for cooking
4 medium onions, roughly chopped
4 cloves garlic, sliced
2 teaspoons sugar
2 teaspoons salt
100 ml/4 fl oz tamarind extract (page 16) *or*
lemon juice
50 g/2 oz chopped fresh coriander leaves
2 tablespoons chopped mint
3 green chillies, chopped
3 tablespoons chopped chives
2 green peppers, deseeded and chopped
orange and lemon slices to garnish

This dish takes about 1 hour 20 minutes to prepare. Rinse the fish and pat it dry with a clean cloth or absorbent kitchen paper.

Heat a little oil in a frying pan. Add the onions and garlic and fry together until transparent. Add the sugar, salt and tamarind extract or lemon juice, then simmer for 5 minutes. Remove the pan from the heat, toss in the chopped coriander, mint, chillies, chives and peppers and mix thoroughly. Stuff the salmon trout with this mixture.

Place the stuffed fish on a large piece of greased foil and smear a little oil over the skin. Wrap the foil around the fish to form an envelope. Lay the package on a baking tray and bake in a moderate oven (180c, 350F, gas 4) for about 1 hour, or until the fish is cooked through. Serve hot, garnished with orange and lemon slices. SERVES 6

Fenugreek Fish

Methi Machi

1 (575-g/1¼-lb) bream or red snapper, cleaned and scaled
6 medium onions, sliced
5 tablespoons oil
3 cloves garlic, chopped
3 green chillies, chopped
⅛ teaspoon turmeric
salt
6 tablespoons chopped fenugreek leaves
150 ml/¼ pint tamarind extract (page 16)
GARNISH
a few small green chillies
a few small lemon wedges

This dish takes about 1 hour to prepare. Slit the fish in half through the middle, leaving the head in place and splitting it too. Remove all the bones from the inside and lay the fish flat, flesh side up, in a large ovenproof dish.

Fry the onions in the oil until golden – do not cook them too quickly or they will burn. Meanwhile, grind the garlic with the chillies and add them to the browned onions with turmeric and salt to taste. Fry for 1 or 2 minutes, then add the fenugreek and cook for a further 2 minutes. Pour in the tamarind extract and cook for 3 minutes.

Spread half the fenugreek mixture over the fish, then turn both pieces over and spread the remaining mixture over the skin side. Cover the fish with cooking foil and bake in a moderately hot oven (190c, 375F, gas 5) for 15 minutes, then uncover the dish and cook for a further 15 to 20 minutes.

Serve immediately, garnished with a few small green chillies – split lengthways several times and soaked in cold water until they curl – and a few small wedges of lemon. SERVES 4

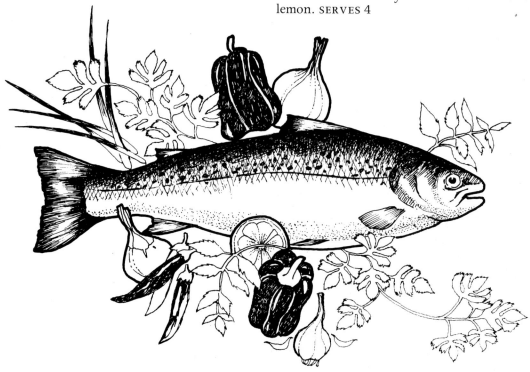

Fish Stuffed with Fresh Herbs, with Plain Rice (page 84), Mixed Vegetable Pickle (page 109) and Deep-fried Snacks (page 98)

Almond Fish

——— Safid Machi ———

50 g/2 oz blanched almonds
50 g/2 oz butter
3 cloves garlic, sliced
4 green chillies, deseeded and finely
sliced into rings
1 (575-g/1¼-lb) bream or red snapper, cleaned and
scaled
salt and pepper
150 ml/¼ pint soured cream

This dish requires 2 hours' soaking time and about 40 minutes' preparation. Soak the almonds in cold water for 2 hours. In a liquidiser, grind the drained nuts with a little water to form a gritty paste.

Melt half the butter on a griddle and fry the garlic for a minute, then add half the chillies and continue to cook. Before the garlic turns brown place the whole fish on the griddle and cook for 7 to 10 minutes.

Mix the ground almond paste with the remaining chillies and spread this mixture over the fish. Dot the remaining butter on top, season with salt and pepper, then grill slowly until the topping browns and the fish is cooked through. Serve immediately, with the soured cream poured over. SERVES 2 TO 4

Baked Fish

——— Dum Ki Machi ———

3 tablespoons sesame seeds
5 tablespoons oil
3 medium onions, sliced
300 ml/½ pint natural yogurt
50 g/2 oz Hara Masala (page 12)
1½ teaspoons Standard Four Spices (page 12)
4 mackerel, cleaned and cut into fillets
salt and pepper
coriander sprigs to garnish

This dish takes about 1 hour to prepare. Roast the sesame seeds in a heavy-based frying pan, then grind them in a coffee grinder. Heat the oil in a frying pan, add the onions and fry until they are soft. Remove from the heat and stir in the yogurt, Hara Masala, ground sesame seeds and Standard Four Spices.

Pour half the mixture into a baking dish. Arrange the mackerel fillets on top, then pour over the remaining mixture and season with salt and pepper. Cover with cooking foil and bake in a moderate oven (180C, 350F, gas 4) for 30 minutes. Remove the foil and cook for a further 20 minutes. When the dish is cooked the excess juices should have dried up. Serve, garnished with coriander sprigs. SERVES 4

Seasoned Fried Fish

—— Tali Machi ——

4 small pieces haddock fillet
1 teaspoon salt
2 large cloves garlic, crushed
1 teaspoon ground ginger
1 teaspoon chilli powder
1 teaspoon turmeric
3 tablespoons ground coriander
4 tablespoons vinegar
oil for deep frying
GARNISH
lemon slices
coriander sprigs

This dish takes about 30 minutes to prepare. Cut the fish fillet lengthways into 2.5-cm/1-in wide pieces. Mix the salt with all the spices and stir in enough vinegar to make a paste. Smear this paste over the fish.

Heat the oil for deep frying to 185C/370F. Fry the pieces of fish, a few at a time, until crisp and golden. Drain on absorbent kitchen paper and serve immediately. The cooked fish has a hot taste. Garnish with lemon slices and coriander. SERVES 4

Steamed Fish in Green Herbs

—— Patheh Ki Machi ——

6 tablespoons white wine vinegar
1 teaspoon salt
2 teaspoons sugar
5 tablespoons desiccated coconut
3 tablespoons chopped fresh coriander leaves
2 tablespoons chopped mint
4 green chillies
6 small pieces haddock
beetroot slices to garnish

This dish takes about 30 minutes to prepare. Put all the ingredients except the fish into a liquidiser and blend together until smooth. Smear this mixture over the fish and wrap each piece individually in cooking foil. It's important that the foil is well sealed so that none of the juices can escape during cooking.

Place the fish packages in a steamer and cook over boiling water for about 20 minutes or until the fillets are cooked. Make sure that the water does not boil dry during cooking and top up with extra boiling water if necessary.

The best way to serve the fish is to give each person a package to unwrap on the plate. This way none of the juices are lost. Garnish each piece of fish with thinly sliced beetroot, cut into diamonds or other shapes.

Note: Patha in Urdu means leaf. Traditionally, the smothered fish in this recipe is wrapped in a leaf: banana leaves are most commonly used. Banana leaves are not too common in the west, so they can be replaced by cooking foil.

Coriander Fish

Kotmir Machi

3 tablespoons oil
1 teaspoon mustard seeds
6 curry leaves
6 tablespoons chopped fresh coriander leaves
3 green chillies
150 ml/$\frac{1}{4}$ pint natural yogurt
675 g/1$\frac{1}{2}$ lb plaice fillets

This dish takes about 25 minutes to prepare. Heat the oil in a frying pan. Add the mustard seeds and curry leaves, then remove the pan from the heat, cover it and leave to cool for 2 minutes.

Meanwhile, purée the chopped coriander, chillies and yogurt in a liquidiser. Arrange the fish fillets in an ovenproof dish and pour the yogurt mixture over them. Handle the fillets carefully to prevent them from breaking up. Top with the spices and oil, adding seasoning to taste. Bake in a moderate oven (180c, 350f, gas 4) for 45 minutes. Serve immediately. SERVES 4 TO 6

Mustard Fish

Machurian

4 teaspoons mustard seeds
pinch of turmeric
salt
575 g/1$\frac{1}{4}$ lb plaice fillets, cut into strips
4 green chillies
25 g/1 oz butter
3 curry leaves, cut into slivers
150 ml/$\frac{1}{4}$ pint water

This dish requires 2 hours' soaking time and it takes about 45 minutes to prepare. Soak 3 teaspoons of the mustard seeds in cold water for 2 hours. Sprinkle the turmeric and salt to taste over the fish and set aside.

Grind the soaked seeds and half the chillies to a fine paste. Melt the butter in a frying pan. Add the remaining mustard seeds, salt and curry leaves and stir well. Place the strips of fish in the pan, cook briefly, then gently turn them over to seal both sides.

Mix the mustard seed paste with the water and pour this over the fish. Cook gently until the liquid is reduced by half – about 10 minutes – then cover the pan and leave over a very low heat for a few minutes before serving. SERVES 4 TO 6

Gingered Halibut and Prawns

—— *Jhinga Machi* ——

4 medium onions, chopped · 6 tablespoons oil
225 g/8 oz halibut fillet
5-cm/2-in piece fresh root ginger
225 g/8 oz peeled cooked prawns · salt
3 green chillies, finely chopped
1 teaspoon ground black pepper
2 green chillies to garnish

This dish takes about 1 hour to prepare. Fry the onions in the oil. When they are transparent, remove three-quarters of them from the pan and set aside. Continue frying the remaining onions until they are golden brown, then remove the pan from the heat.

Skin the fish if you like, then cut it into 2.5-cm/1-in chunks and finely slice the ginger. Spread the lightly cooked onions in the base of an ovenproof casserole dish and top with the ginger. Mix the prawns, fish and salt to taste and arrange the mixture over the ginger. Sprinkle the finely chopped chillies and ground black pepper over the fish and top with the browned onions with any oil from the pan. Cover the casserole and bake in a moderate oven (180c, 350f, gas 4) for 45 minutes.

The cooked dish will be fairly hot, with a sweet flavour from the onions and the zesty aroma of ginger. Serve immediately. Garnish with green chillies, cut lengthways into strips. SERVES 4

Crab-stuffed Aubergines

—— *Baigan Khekra* ——

3 small firm aubergines · salt and pepper
2 tablespoons oil · 1 small onion, chopped
1 teaspoon Standard Four Spices (page 12)
3 tablespoons tomato purée
juice of 1 lemon · 225 g/8 oz crabmeat
25 g/1 oz butter · 75 g/3 oz semolina
chopped fresh coriander leaves to garnish

This dish takes about 40 minutes to prepare. Cut the aubergines in half lengthways. Remove all the flesh from the aubergines, but do not damage the skins. The best way to do this is to cut through the flesh in both directions, then use a grapefruit knife or spoon to scoop out the pieces. Chop the flesh to a pulp and set aside. Place the shells in cold water and add 1 tablespoon salt.

Heat the oil in a frying pan. Fry the chopped onion with the Standard Four Spices. Add the aubergine pulp and sauté for a few minutes, then stir in the tomato purée and continue to cook for another 5 minutes. Pour in the lemon juice and add salt and pepper to taste. Remove the pan from the heat, then mix in half the crabmeat.

Drain and dry the aubergine shells and place about 2 tablespoons of the crab mixture in each shell. Top each with a layer of the remaining crabmeat, then spoon in the rest of the stuffing. Melt the butter and brush a little over each shell. Sprinkle the semolina generously over the top of the aubergines to form a crusty layer, adding a little salt and pepper. Bake in a moderately hot oven (200c, 400f, gas 6) for 25 to 30 minutes. Serve immediately, garnished with chopped coriander. SERVES 3 TO 6

Hot Tempered Prawns

Baghare Jhingeh

¼ teaspoon turmeric
1½ teaspoons chilli powder
1 teaspoon salt
2 tablespoons vinegar
450 g/1 lb shelled uncooked king prawns
3 tablespoons oil
1 teaspoon kalonji
4 cloves garlic, sliced
4 dried red chillies
6 curry leaves

This dish takes about 25 minutes to prepare. Mix the turmeric, chilli powder and salt with the vinegar and pour this mixture over the prawns, mixing thoroughly to coat all the prawns in the spices.

Heat the oil in a medium-sized saucepan, remove from the heat, then add the kalonji, garlic, chillies and curry leaves, cover the pan and allow the spices to cool for 2 minutes.

Add the prawns and cook over a medium heat, stirring continuously, for about 10 minutes. Reduce the heat and cover the pan, then leave for 5 minutes before serving. These prawns are very hot in flavour. SERVES 4 TO 6

Note: Uncooked king prawns are available fresh from good fishmongers, and they are also sold frozen with their shells removed.

Green Fenugreek Prawns

Hareh Jhingeh

4 tablespoons oil
2 bunches spring onions, trimmed and sliced
3 green chillies, finely sliced
2½ teaspoons Standard Four Spices (page 12)
450 g/1 lb peeled cooked prawns
1 teaspoon salt
½ bunch fenugreek leaves, trimmed and chopped
4 tomatoes, sliced, to garnish

This dish takes about 30 minutes to prepare. Heat the oil in a saucepan, add the spring onions and chillies and cook for a few minutes. Add the Standard Four Spices and cook, stirring continuously, for about 2 minutes.

Stir in the prawns, salt and chopped fenugreek, cover the pan and cook gently for 20 minutes. At the end of this cooking time reduce the heat to a very low setting and leave the prawns for a few minutes before serving.

Arrange the tomato slices around the edge of a serving dish and pile the prawns in the middle, then serve immediately. SERVES 4

Note: This is a dry dish of prawns smothered in a fenugreek paste: it is sharp and hot in flavour.

Shrimps with Spinach

—— Palak Jhingeh ——

225 g/8 oz dried shrimps
2 medium onions, sliced
3 tablespoons oil
1 teaspoon finely chopped garlic
½ teaspoon finely chopped fresh root ginger
¼ teaspoon salt
450 g/1 lb fresh spinach, trimmed and shredded
4 green chillies, chopped
2 tablespoons Hara Masala (page 12)
1 white radish to garnish

This dish requires 30 minutes' soaking time and it takes about 30 minutes to prepare. Rinse the shrimps under cold running water, then soak them in cold water to cover for at least half an hour.

Fry the onions in the oil until lightly browned. Add the garlic, ginger and salt, and cook, stirring continuously, for a few minutes. Stir in the drained shrimps and spinach, cover the pan and cook over medium to low heat for about 20 to 30 minutes or until the shrimps are tender. Stir once or twice during cooking. The liquid from the spinach should be sufficient to tenderise the shrimps, but extra water may be added if necessary.

Stir in the chopped chillies and Hara Masala, then reduce the heat to very low, cover the pan and leave for about 10 minutes.

Slice the radish into one long, spiral strip. Arrange the shrimps on a serving dish and garnish with the radish spiral. SERVES 4

Note: Dried shrimps are obtainable from Indian and Chinese food stores and some delicatessens. Before cooking they must be soaked for at least 30 minutes in tepid water otherwise they become leathery. They are usually salted, so season the dish carefully.

Spiced King Prawns

—— Jhingeh Tomate ——

1.25 kg/2½ lb peeled uncooked king prawns
150 ml/¼ pint oil
5 medium onions, sliced
3 large cloves garlic, crushed
1 teaspoon ground ginger
½ teaspoon turmeric
1½ teaspoons chilli powder
1 teaspoon salt
1 kg/2 lb tomatoes, chopped
12 curry leaves
100 ml/4 fl oz vinegar
2 teaspoons sugar
2 green chillies, slit lengthways

This dish takes about 1¼ hours to prepare. Rinse the prawns quickly in cold water but do not soak them or some of the flavour will be lost. Lay the prawns on absorbent kitchen paper to dry.

Heat the oil in a large heavy-based frying pan and quickly fry the prawns, a few at a time, to seal them. As soon as they stiffen and curl remove them from the pan and set aside. Add the onions and cook until transparent, then add the garlic, ginger, turmeric, chilli powder and salt to the oil remaining in the pan. Cook, stirring continuously, for a few minutes. Add the tomatoes and curry leaves. Continue to cook over a high heat for about 10 to 15 minutes, or until the excess liquid has evaporated and a thick tomato sauce remains. Replace the prawns in the sauce and cook for about 10 minutes.

Stir in the vinegar, sugar and green chillies and leave, covered, over low heat for 10 minutes. Serve hot. SERVES 4 TO 6

Chicken dishes

The era of the frozen 'batteried' chickens has not yet reached Hyderabad. Animals are sold in the *chowk* or animal bazaar. Some animals are sold for pets; others, like the chickens, are carried off home, fattened and killed. In the bazaar, the chickens are kept in a large dome made of cane called a *jhamp*.

One day when the servants were off duty, Zuju surprised her sister by killing the chicken for the evening meal. She walked out of the house, with two dead chickens in either hand and her sister passed out on the spot. This was not the sort of work for a lady!

Before cooking, the chickens are usually divided into seven or eight pieces: two legs, two wings, two thighs and one or two pieces of breast. The best chicken is a small one because there is little fat on the bird. The chicken should be skinned, or partially skinned, before cooking so that the spices can impregnate the meat.

Clockwise from the top: Baked Chicken in Saffron (page 36), Shredded Chicken and Chicken Smothered in Ginger (both overleaf)

Red Pepper Chicken

— *Lal Murgi* —

150 ml/¼ pint oil
4 cloves garlic, chopped
1 kg/2 lb tomatoes, chopped
1 tablespoon cumin seeds
1 teaspoon salt
1 small oven-ready roasting chicken, jointed *or*
4 chicken joints
1 medium beetroot, cooked and chopped
1 red pepper, deseeded and chopped
a few small whole red peppers to garnish (optional)

This dish takes about 1 to 1¼ hours to cook. Heat the oil in a saucepan and toss in the garlic. Sauté the garlic for a few minutes, then add the tomatoes, cumin seeds and salt. Cook until the tomato pulp is reduced by half.

Meanwhile, lay the chicken pieces on a large piece of cooking foil in a roasting tin. Add the beetroot and chopped red pepper to the tomato mixture and spoon it evenly over the joints. Wrap the foil around the chicken and cook in a moderately hot oven (190c, 375f, gas 5) for 40 to 60 minutes. When the chicken is cooked all the juices should have dried up. Serve, garnished with small whole red peppers if you like. SERVES 4

Shredded Chicken

— *Kurgi Murgi* —

4 tablespoons oil
2 bunches spring onions, chopped
3 green chillies, chopped
1 teaspoon chopped fresh root ginger
2 cloves garlic, chopped
8 small chicken pieces, skinned
1½ teaspoons salt
150 ml/¼ pint water
150 ml/¼ pint natural yogurt
300 ml/½ pint soured cream
1 teaspoon ground black pepper
1 or 2 spring onions, shredded lengthways

This dish takes about 1½ hours to prepare. Heat the oil in a flameproof casserole or frying pan which has a lid, add the spring onions and chillies and fry them until they are bruised, then add the ginger, garlic and chicken pieces. Cook for a few minutes to seal the meat. Sprinkle the salt over the chicken and pour in the water. Cover the pan and simmer for 30 to 40 minutes or until the chicken is tender.

Remove the chicken from the pan and strip all the meat off the bone, then shred it into strips. Place the chicken in an ovenproof dish. Mix the yogurt, soured cream and pepper with the liquid remaining in the pan and pour the mixture over the chicken. Bake in a moderate oven (180c, 350f, gas 4) for 30 minutes. Serve immediately, garnished with shredded spring onions. SERVES 4 TO 6

Chicken Smothered in Ginger

— *Adrak Murgi* —

1 small oven-ready roasting chicken
5-cm/2-in piece fresh root ginger
4 green chillies
150 ml/¼ pint oil
3 medium onions, chopped
1½ teaspoons salt
300 ml/½ pint water
GARNISH
quartered lime slices
1 or 2 green chillies

This dish takes about 1 hour to prepare. Neatly skin and joint the chicken into small pieces. Peel and finely slice the ginger and cut the chillies lengthways into thin slivers.

Heat the oil and add 4 or 5 slices of ginger and a sprinkling of chillies. Add the chicken pieces, two or three at a time, and cook quickly, turning them over once or twice, to seal the meat. The chicken should not be allowed to brown. Remove the joints from the pan and set aside.

Now add the onions and fry them until they are transparent. Put a little more ginger and chillies in the pan, add the salt and replace the chicken. Pour in the water. Bring to the boil, then cover and cook slowly until the chicken is tender – about 15 to 20 minutes. At the end of the cooking time increase the heat and uncover the pan. Continue to cook, stirring the ingredients and turning the chicken frequently, adding further sprinklings of chilli and ginger from time to time.

When most of the liquid has evaporated and the cooked chicken pieces are well glazed in the spices, add any remaining ginger and chillies. Serve immediately, garnished with quartered lime slices and the chillies, shredded from the stalk end to make tassles as shown in the picture. SERVES 4

Red Pepper Chicken, Crab-stuffed Aubergines (page 27), Hyderabadi Dal (page 66) and Two-layered Bread (page 98)

Baked Chicken

———— Dum Ki Murgi ————

2 tablespoons poppy seeds
4 tablespoons oil
2 medium onions, finely sliced
300 ml/½ pint natural yogurt
4 green chillies
1 teaspoon Garam Masala (page 13)
1 teaspoon salt
6 chicken joints
GARNISH
chopped fresh coriander leaves
a few radishes

This dish requires 2 hours' marinating time and about 2 hours' preparation. Roast and grind the poppy seeds. Heat the oil in a frying pan, add the onions and cook until golden brown. Mix the onions with the yogurt, poppy seeds, chillies, Garam Masala and salt, then blend in a liquidiser until smooth. Skin the chicken pieces and place them in a dish. Pour the yogurt mixture over the chicken and leave to marinate for at least two hours.

Lay a large piece of cooking foil in a roasting tin. Place the chicken with its marinade on the foil and fold up the edges to form an envelope, sealing the edges well. Bake in a moderate oven (180C, 350F, gas 4) for 1 hour.

Open the foil and continue cooking for a further 15 minutes until all the excess juices have evaporated. Serve immediately, garnished with the chopped coriander and radishes. SERVES 6

Chicken Hara Masala

———— Hari Murgi ————

6 chicken joints
50 g/2 oz Hara Masala (page 12)
150 ml/¼ pint natural yogurt
1½ teaspoons salt
about 25 g/1 oz butter
GARNISH
lime slices
mint sprigs

This dish takes about 1¾ hours to prepare. Skin the chicken pieces. Blend the Hara Masala and yogurt together in a liquidiser. Place the chicken pieces on a large piece of cooking foil in a roasting tin, then spread the green yogurt mixture all over the chicken. Season with the salt, dot with the butter and bake in a moderate oven (180C, 350F, gas 4) for 1¼ hours.

Open the foil and cook for a further 15 minutes to reduce the juices. Serve the chicken arranged on a heated serving dish and garnished with the slices of lime and sprigs of mint. SERVES 6

Tandoori Chicken

———— Tanduri Murgi ————

2 cloves
6 small dried red chillies
300 ml/½ pint natural yogurt
1½ teaspoons salt
½ teaspoon powdered red food colouring
1 teaspoon ground ginger
2 cloves garlic, crushed
1½ teaspoons chilli powder
4–6 small chicken joints, skinned
25 g/1 oz butter
GARNISH
lemon wedges
a few green chillies, finely sliced
salad ingredients

This dish requires overnight marinating and about 1 hour's preparation. In a small saucepan roast the cloves and dried red chillies, bruising the chillies with a wooden spoon, until the aroma is released. Grind all these ingredients together as finely as possible.

Mix the yogurt, salt, food colouring, ground ginger, garlic and chilli powder with the ground ingredients. Place the chicken pieces in a dish and pour the yogurt mixture over. Leave to marinate overnight.

Smear the butter over a large piece of cooking foil. Arrange the chicken on the foil with the marinade and dot any remaining butter on top. Fold the foil around the chicken, sealing the edges well. Bake in a moderately hot oven (200 c, 400 f, gas 6) for 40 minutes. At the end of the cooking time remove the chicken from the oven, open the foil and cook under a hot grill until all the juices have dried up. Serve immediately, garnished with lemon wedges, a few green chilli slices and salad ingredients (for example, shredded lettuce and cucumber). SERVES 4 TO 6

Spicy Fried Chicken

———— Tikka ————

1 oven-ready roasting chicken, cut into
about 12 small joints
1 medium onion, chopped
3 green chillies
1 bunch fresh coriander leaves, trimmed
juice of 1 lemon
2 cloves
1½ teaspoons salt
½ teaspoon ground black pepper
2 teaspoons Standard Four Spices (page 12)
oil for deep frying
GARNISH
1 tomato, cut into wedges
coriander sprigs

This dish takes about 30 to 50 minutes to prepare. The chicken in this recipe is deep fried, so it is important that the pieces are small enough to cook thoroughly. Ask your butcher to chop up the chicken if you like.

Grind the onion, chillies, coriander, lemon juice and cloves to a smooth paste. Add the salt, pepper and Standard Four Spices and smear this mixture over the chicken pieces. Heat the oil for deep frying to 185 c/ 370 f. Fry the chicken in the oil until very well browned. Drain on absorbent kitchen paper and serve immediately, garnished with tomato wedges and coriander sprigs. SERVES 4 TO 6

Baked Chicken in Saffron

———— *Zafrani Murgi* ————

$\frac{1}{4}$ teaspoon saffron strands
150 ml/$\frac{1}{4}$ pint boiling water
50 g/2 oz butter
1 small oven-ready roasting chicken, skinned
$\frac{1}{2}$ teaspoon salt
STUFFING
100 g/4 oz dried apricots
1 lemon
1 orange
1 tablespoon raisins
1 tablespoon sultanas
2 or 3 dried red chillies
3 tablespoons oil
3 cloves garlic, finely sliced
15 small pickling onions
salt
coriander sprigs to garnish (optional)

This dish takes about 2 hours to prepare. First pound the saffron, then add the boiling water and set aside. Now prepare the stuffing: soak the apricots in cold water to cover for 1 hour. Halve both the lemon and the orange and squeeze out the juice from the fruit. Place the raisins and sultanas in a bowl and pour over the fruit juice, then set aside to soak.

Scrape away and discard all the flesh and excess pith from the inside of the fruit shells and place them in a bowl. Pour in enough boiling water to cover the shells and leave to soak for 2 to 3 minutes. Drain the skins and allow to cool until they can be handled. Scrape or cut all the pith from inside and finely shred the translucent peel.

Using scissors, cut the chillies into fine rings. Heat the oil in a small saucepan and add the chillies with the garlic. Cook until the garlic is lightly browned, then add the pickling onions and cook, covered, for 5 minutes. Drain and roughly chop the apricots, then add them to the onions with the raisin and sultana mixture (with the juices from soaking) and 2 tablespoons of the saffron liquid. Stir in salt to taste and cook gently until the liquid has reduced and the mixture is dry enough to use as a stuffing.

Melt the butter in a small saucepan. Stuff the chicken with the prepared mixture and tie it neatly into shape. Place the chicken on a large piece of cooking foil in a roasting tin, then brush half the remaining saffron water over the top and sprinkle with the salt. Arrange any remaining stuffing around the bird and sprinkle the orange and lemon rind over the breast. Pour the butter over the bird, then fold the foil around the chicken and close it neatly to keep in all the flavour. Place in a moderately hot oven (190c, 375f, gas 5) and cook for 1 to 1$\frac{1}{4}$ hours. Open the foil and continue to cook for a further 15 to 20 minutes or until the chicken is cooked, basting it frequently with the saffron juices.

Immediately before serving, pour the remaining saffron liquid over the chicken; the aroma of the saffron will be pronounced. Garnish with coriander sprigs, if you like, and arrange any extra stuffing round the chicken.
SERVES 4

Sour Lime Chicken

Nimboo Aur Murgi

2 dried limes
6 tablespoons oil
12 curry leaves
1 small oven-ready roasting chicken, jointed into
small pieces
2 medium onions, sliced
2 cloves garlic, chopped
$\frac{1}{2}$ teaspoon chopped fresh root ginger
$\frac{1}{4}$ teaspoon turmeric
1 teaspoon chilli powder
3 tablespoons tomato purée
1$\frac{1}{2}$ teaspoons salt
1 tablespoon chopped green pepper

This dish requires 2 hours' soaking time and 1 hour to prepare. Using a sharp pointed knife make two holes in the dried limes, then soak them in 450 ml/$\frac{3}{4}$ pint cold water for at least 2 hours. Place another bowl or saucer on top to prevent the fruit from floating. Fresh limes are not used in this dish as they give a bitter taste.

Heat the oil with a few curry leaves – four or five. Add the chicken pieces, two or three at a time and fry quickly, turning the pieces frequently, to seal them on all sides. Remove from the pan and set aside.

In the same oil, fry the onions until they are transparent. Immediately add the garlic, ginger, turmeric and chilli powder and cook, stirring continuously, for 2 to 3 minutes. Add the tomato purée, the remaining curry leaves, the soaked limes (with their soaking water) and salt. Return the chicken pieces to the pan and continue to cook for 5 minutes. You can now transfer the contents of the pan to an ovenproof casserole dish and finish cooking in a moderate oven (180c, 350F, gas 4) for 45 minutes. Alternatively, continue cooking over a low heat for about 45 minutes or until the chicken is cooked.

Add the chopped green pepper and leave the pan, covered, over very low heat, or in the turned-off oven, for a few minutes. Serve hot. SERVES 4 TO 6

Note: Dried limes (illustrated on page 17) can be obtained from Indian shops and Chinese supermarkets. They are small, brown and hard, and require fairly lengthy soaking before they can be cooked. They give the completed dish a pronounced and excellent flavour, so the preparation which is required is worthwhile.

The dry limes can be stored for several months in an airtight bag or container in a cool, dry place, so when you find a shop that sells them it is well worth buying a few packets.

Chicken Vindaloo

Vindaloo

1½ teaspoons ground coriander
1½ teaspoon ground cumin
¼ teaspoon kalonji
¼ teaspoon fenugreek seeds
¼ teaspoon mustard seeds
1 teaspoon aniseeds
2.5-cm/1-in piece cinnamon stick · 3 cloves
¾ teaspoon ground black pepper
2 tablespoons desiccated coconut
2 tablespoons unsalted peanuts
150 ml/¼ pint vinegar
2 small cloves garlic, crushed
¾ teaspoon chopped fresh root ginger
½ teaspoon turmeric
1½ teaspoons chilli powder · 2 teaspoon salt
1 small oven-ready roasting chicken, skinned and
chopped into 6 to 8 pieces
150 ml/¼ pint oil · 12 curry leaves
1 teaspoon cumin seeds
300 ml/½ pint water
chopped coriander leaves to garnish

*This dish requires overnight marinating and about 1½ hours'
preparation.* Roast and grind the first eleven ingredients.
Mix in the vinegar, garlic, ginger, turmeric and chilli
powder. Stir in the salt and spread the mixture over the
chicken pieces. Leave to marinate overnight.

Heat the oil in a flameproof casserole, then add the
curry leaves and cumin seeds. Cook for a few minutes,
add the chicken and cook, turning once or twice, for 15
minutes. Cover and continue cooking until the chicken is
tender – about 30 to 40 minutes. Add the water and heat
through. Cover the casserole and leave over a very low
heat for a few minutes before serving, garnished with the
chopped coriander. SERVES 4 TO 6

Fried Chicken

Karhai Murg

6 tablespoons oil
1 small onion, very finely chopped
½ teaspoon turmeric
1 teaspoon ground coriander
1 teaspoon ground cumin
1 teaspoon chilli powder
2 tablespoons water
1 small oven-ready roasting chicken, jointed
675 g/1½ lb tomatoes, chopped
salt
1 teaspoon coriander seeds
4–6 cloves garlic, chopped
4 or 5 green chillies, chopped

GARNISH
2 tomatoes, quartered
coriander sprigs

This dish takes about 1 hour to prepare. Heat the oil in a
karhai (Indian wok), heavy-based saucepan or flameproof casserole. Add the onion and fry until transparent.
Mix the turmeric, ground coriander, ground cumin and
chilli powder with the water. Stir this spice mixture into
the onions and cook until the liquid has dried up – about
3 to 4 minutes. Add the chicken pieces and fry on all
sides, then add the tomatoes and salt to taste. Cover
closely (place a weight on the lid if it is loose) and cook for
15 minutes.

At the end of the cooking time add the coriander seeds,
garlic and chillies. Cook, uncovered, until all the tomato
juices have evaporated, then continue frying until the
chicken is well glazed and the tomatoes have disintegrated. Serve from the karhai or pan or transfer the chicken
to a serving dish and garnish with the tomatoes and
coriander. SERVES 4 TO 6

Walnut Chicken

— Fezun Jun —

4 tablespoons oil
2 medium onions, finely sliced
100 g/4 oz walnuts, roughly ground
1 small oven-ready roasting chicken, jointed
300 ml/½ pint water
1 teaspoon salt
2.5-cm/1-in piece cinnamon stick
150 ml/¼ pint tamarind extract
6 curry leaves
2 teaspoons sugar

This dish takes about 45 to 50 minutes to prepare. Heat the oil in a pan large enough to hold the chicken pieces without having them overlapping. Fry the sliced onions until transparent, then add the ground walnuts and continue cooking, stirring constantly, for 3 to 4 minutes, or until the onions mix with the walnuts to make a paste. Remove this mixture from the pan, squeezing out as much oil as possible.

Cook the chicken in the oil left in the pan until the pieces are well sealed on all sides. Return the paste to the pan, pour in the water, then add the salt and the cinnamon. Cook, covered, for about 15 to 20 minutes, or until the chicken is cooked. Pour in the tamarind extract, then toss in the curry leaves and sugar. Uncover the pan and continue to cook gently for a further 5 minutes. Re-cover the pan and leave over a low heat for 10 minutes before serving. SERVES 4 TO 6

Aromatic Chicken with Yogurt Sauce

— Murgi Ka Khorma —

2 tablespoons poppy seeds
1 tablespoon chirongi nuts or almonds
5 tablespoons oil
2 medium onions, finely sliced
150 ml/¼ pint natural yogurt
2 tablespoons Hara Masala (page 12)
1 teaspoon Garam Masala (page 13)
450 ml/¾ pint water · 25 g/1 oz butter
1 small oven-ready roasting chicken, jointed
1 tablespoon ground coriander
2 teaspoons Standard Four Spices (page 12)
1½ teaspoons salt
coriander sprigs to garnish

This dish takes about 1 to 1½ hours to prepare. Roast and grind the poppy seeds with the chirongi nuts or almonds. Heat half the oil in a frying pan, add the onions and cook until they are golden brown. Set aside to drain on absorbent kitchen paper. Reserve a few onions for garnish, then place the remainder in a liquidiser with the yogurt, poppy seeds and nuts, Hara Masala, Garam Masala and half the water. Blend until smooth.

Heat the remaining oil and butter in a large flameproof casserole and fry the chicken joints briefly to seal in their flavour. Remove and set aside. Add the coriander, Standard Four Spices and salt to the pan, then cook, stirring continuously, for 3 minutes or until the coriander is well fried. Pour in the blended mixture and the remaining water, heat through and replace the chicken. Cook in a moderate oven (180C, 350F, gas 4) for 45 to 60 minutes. The flavour of the spices should penetrate the chicken and the sauce should have thickened at the end of the cooking time. Garnish with the reserved onions and coriander sprigs, and serve hot. SERVES 4 TO 6

Meat dishes

It is not unknown for an Indian, even a Hyderabadi, to refuse to cook beef. The reason, of course, is that the cow is sacred and the eating of beef is against the tenets of the Hindu religion. While lamb is used for dishes prepared in a sauce, the more strongly flavoured mutton is used for mince and kabaabs. Mutton is difficult to find in Britain, so beef can be used for kabaabs and mince dishes.

It is generally thought that kabaab describes pieces of meat cooked on a skewer over charcoal: this is correct, but it is also used to describe the preparation of meat in a dry fashion. So kabaab may be finely minced meat, shaped into cutlets, and baked slices of meat as well as the well-known chunks grilled on skewers. Lean beef is always used.

Lamb is often cooked on the bone. This adds flavour to the dish and the marrow helps to thicken the gravy. The lamb has to be chopped into small pieces and your butcher will have no trouble in doing this for you. In India, mutton is generally minced for kabaabs, but lamb is better.

Mince is highly versatile, it cooks quickly, freezes well and goes with practically everything. It's economical and it is the perfect meat for newcomers to Indian food to experiment on. Cooked mince should not be frozen with too much oil. To be sure of getting good mince, choose chuck, braising or stewing steak and ask the butcher to mince it twice for you. If you can't be bothered to go to this trouble the mince you cook will probably be very greasy and the meat won't absorb the spices so easily.

This chapter also contains a few recipes for liver and kidneys. Only lamb's liver is used. Any veins should be removed and the liver should be rinsed before cooking. It is almost always used in fine thin slivers. Similarly, lamb's kidneys should always be used and these should be cut in half in order to remove the veins, then thoroughly washed and rinsed before cooking. Kidneys are quick and easy to prepare and excellent if you're in a hurry.

From the top left: Soured Lamb with Aubergines, Succulent Lamb with Potatoes (both overleaf) and Hyderabadi-style Chops (page 44)

Soured Lamb with Aubergines

———— Baigan Ka Musamma ————

4 small aubergines · 3½ teaspoons salt
2 medium onions, sliced · 6 tablespoons oil
2 teaspoons Standard Four Spices (page 12)
450 g/1 lb lean leg of lamb, cubed
600 ml/1 pint water · oil for deep frying
juice of 3 lemons
2 tablespoons Hara Masala (page 12)

This dish takes about 1 hour to prepare. Carefully peel the aubergines, leaving the stalks intact. If the aubergines are small and tender the peel may be left on. Cut each aubergine lengthways into two halves. Place the halved aubergines flat on a chopping board and make three or four cuts from just below the stalk. Cut outward from the stalk so that the separated strips of aubergine form a fan-shape. Soak in cold water to cover, with 2 teaspoons salt added, for about 15 minutes. This prevents discoloration.

While the aubergines are soaking, fry the onion slices in the oil in a large flameproof casserole until golden. Remove a few and drain these on absorbent kitchen paper; reserve for the garnish. Add the Standard Four Spices to the onions in the pan. Cook, stirring continuously, then add the meat with the remaining salt and continue cooking, stirring, until the meat is well sealed. Pour in the water, bring to the boil, then cover and cook slowly for 30 minutes.

While the meat is cooking remove the soaked aubergine fans from the water and dab them dry. Heat the oil for deep frying to 185c/370F. Deep fry the aubergines, preferably individually, until golden. When cooked, drain them on absorbent kitchen paper.

When the meat is thoroughly cooked, slide the aubergines gently into the pan. Hold the stalks and take care the aubergines don't break up. Cover the pan and leave over low heat for about 15 minutes so that the flavours are well mingled. Remove the pan from the heat, pour the lemon juice over the meat and aubergines and garnish with the reserved onions and Hara Masala. Serve hot. SERVES 4

Leg of Lamb Baked with Saffron

———— Zaafrani Raan ————

1 teaspoon saffron strands
450 ml/¾ pint boiling water
1 (1.5-kg/3-lb) leg of lamb
300 ml/½ pint natural yogurt · 2 teaspoons salt
½ teaspoon ground black pepper
6 cloves garlic, crushed
6 green chillies, chopped · 25 g/1 oz butter

This dish takes about 1¾ hours to prepare. Pound the saffron and mix it with the boiling water. Set aside. Trim all the fat from the joint. Mix the yogurt, salt, pepper,

garlic and chillies with a quarter of the saffron. Smear this mixture and the butter over the joint, then wrap it in cooking foil, to enclose all the juices. Bake in a moderately hot oven (200c, 400F, gas 6) for 1 hour.

Unwrap the foil and pour another quarter of the saffron over the meat. Continue cooking for a further 15 minutes, again wrapped in foil. Open the foil and bake for a final 20 minutes. Shortly before serving, pour the remaining saffron over the meat. SERVES 6

Succulent Lamb with Potatoes

———— Aloo Ka Khorma ————

¼ teaspoon saffron strands
3 tablespoons boiling water
675 g/1½ lb lamb, chopped into small pieces from the leg (with bone)
300 ml/½ pint natural yogurt · salt
3 cloves garlic, crushed
1 teaspoon chopped fresh root ginger
1 teaspoon chilli powder · ¼ teaspoon turmeric
5 almonds · 1 teaspoon poppy seeds
1 teaspoon chirongi nuts · 6 tablespoons oil
4 medium onions, sliced · 2 cloves · 3 cardamoms
2.5-cm/1-in piece cinnamon stick
2 teaspoons ground coriander · 450 ml/¾ pint water
3 medium potatoes
3 green chillies · 3 or 4 fresh coriander sprigs
3 or 4 mint sprigs · ½ teaspoon chopped mint
½ teaspoon Garam Masala (page 13)

This dish requires at least 1 hour to marinate and 1 hour's preparation. Pound the saffron and mix it with the 3 tablespoons boiling water. Place the lamb in a dish, then pour in the yogurt and add salt to taste with the garlic, ginger, chilli powder and turmeric. Cover and leave to marinate for at least an hour. Roast and grind together the poppy seeds, chirongi nuts and almonds.

Heat the oil in a large frying pan or flameproof casserole. Add the onions and fry them until golden. Remove the slices from the pan and drain them on absorbent kitchen paper. Reserve some of the onions for garnish, then blend the remainder in a liquidiser with enough water to make a paste. Add the cloves, cardamoms and cinnamon stick to the oil remaining in the pan and fry for 1 to 2 minutes. Add the meat, with its marinade, and cook until the liquid evaporates. Stir occasionally.

Sprinkle the ground coriander over the meat and cook, stirring all the time, for a few minutes. Now pour in the water and add the ground poppy seeds and nuts. Bring to the boil, then cook gently for about 30 minutes. Quarter the potatoes lengthways and add these to the meat. Cover the pan and cook gently for a further 15 minutes. Add the whole chillies, coriander and mint sprigs, fried onion purée and the saffron. Cover and cook gently until the potatoes are tender. Sprinkle the Garam Masala and chopped mint over the khorma. Serve hot, garnished with the reserved onions. SERVES 4

Clockwise from the top: Gram Soured Rice (page 84), Leg of Lamb Baked with Saffron, White Lentil Fritters served in yogurt (page 100) and Zebra Potatoes (page 59)

Lamb and Potato with Fenugreek

— *Aloo Methi Gosht* —

2 medium onions, sliced
6 tablespoons oil
2½ teaspoons Standard Four Spices (page 12)
675 g/1½ lb leg or shoulder of lamb, cut into small
pieces (with the bone)
450 ml/¾ pint water
1½ teaspoons salt
6 tablespoons chopped fenugreek leaves
4 medium potatoes *or* 4 small turnips, diced
2 green chillies, chopped

This dish takes about 1½ hours to prepare. Fry the onions in
the oil in a flameproof casserole until golden. Add the
Standard Four Spices and continue to cook, stirring all the
time. Drop the small pieces of meat into the pan and
continue cooking for a few minutes to seal the meat. Pour
in the water and add the salt, then bring to the boil.
Lower the heat, cover the pan and continue simmering for
about 30 to 40 minutes or until the meat is tender.

Now add the fenugreek leaves and the diced potatoes
or turnips, then cook for a further 15 minutes until the
vegetables are tender. Sprinkle the chopped chillies over
the meat and potatoes and leave over a low heat, covered,
for a few minutes. Serve hot. SERVES 4 TO 6

Note: There are two versions of this recipe. One uses
turnip and this one uses potato. Turnip is used in the
same proportions as potato, but the final Shaljam Methi
Gosht has a completely different flavour to the potato
version.

Hyderabadi-style Chops

— *Chaaps* —

6 lamb chops
1 teaspoon salt
1 teaspoon Standard Four Spices (page 12)
1 tablespoon vinegar
2 tablespoons oil
1 teaspoon ground black pepper
tomato slices to garnish
GARNISH
tomato slices
white radish slices, cut into shapes

This dish takes about 30 minutes to prepare. Trim all the fat
and gristle from the chops. Mix the salt and Standard Four
Spices with the vinegar and smear the mixture over the
chops.

Brush the chops with oil, sprinkle them with black
pepper and arrange them on a rack in a grill pan. Cook
under a hot grill until lightly browned on both sides and
cooked through. Serve hot, arranged neatly on a heated
serving dish and garnished with the slices of tomato and
white radish shapes. SERVES 3 TO 6

Lamb with Spinach

—— Palak Gosht ——

2 medium onions, sliced
6 tablespoons oil
¾ teaspoon ground ginger
2 cloves garlic, crushed
1 teaspoon salt
450 g/1 lb leg of lamb, diced (with the bone)
300 ml/½ pint water
450 g/1 lb fresh spinach, trimmed
6 tablespoons finely chopped fresh coriander leaves
1 teaspoon dill weed
2 tablespoons natural yogurt
2 green chillies, chopped

This dish takes about 1¼ hours to prepare. Fry the sliced onions in the oil in a flameproof casserole until lightly browned. Then add the ginger, garlic, salt and meat and cook, stirring all the time, for 2 to 3 minutes. Add the water, bring to the boil and cook for 30 to 40 minutes or until the meat is nearly tender.

Stir in the spinach and continue to cook, covered, for 10 minutes. Reduce the heat and mix in the chopped coriander, dill, yogurt and chillies. Leave, covered, over a low heat for 10 minutes. The dish should be fairly dry, if not cook, uncovered, to reduce to a thick sauce. Serve hot. SERVES 4

Note: The best meat for this dish is that which is cut from the lower end of the leg. There is a little work involved in removing all the tendons but this is repaid by the end result. The number of green chillies that are used determine how hot the dish will end up.

Piquant Tomato Lamb

—— Tomate Ka Do Pyaza ——

6 tablespoons oil
675 g/1½ lb breast of lamb, diced (with the bone)
4 medium onions, sliced
3 teaspoons Standard Four Spices (page 12)
1½ teaspoons salt
450 ml/¾ pint water
1 kg/2 lb firm tomatoes, chopped
12 curry leaves
3 green chillies

This dish requires about 1¼ hours' preparation. Heat the oil in a saucepan, then add the meat, onions, Standard Four Spices, salt and water. Bring to the boil, reduce the heat and cover the pan, then cook for about 30 to 40 minutes, or until the meat is tender.

Now add the tomatoes and curry leaves and cook, uncovered, for 10 minutes until some of the liquid has evaporated and the tomatoes form a thick sauce. Throw in the whole green chillies, cover the pan and leave over a very low heat for 10 minutes. Serve hot. SERVES 4

Note: The standing time, or *dum-dena*, at the end of the cooking time for the breast of lamb, is most important for bringing out the full flavour of the meat and all the goodness from the bone. It is also during the *dum-dena* that the flavour of the spices penetrates the meat.

Ground Meat Kabaabs

———— Seekh Ke Kabaabs ————

1 medium onion, chopped
1 tablespoons besan flour
1 teaspoon ground cumin
1 teaspoon chirongi nuts
6 almonds · 1 teaspoon poppy seeds
450 g/1 lb lean braising steak
½ teaspoon papaya pulp or meat tenderiser
(optional)
½ teaspoon salt · 1 large clove garlic, crushed
½ teaspoon ground ginger
1 teaspoon ground green chillies
1 tablespoon lime juice
1 teaspoon Garam Masala (page 13)
1 egg · 1 tablespoon oil

This dish takes about 1 hour to prepare. Cook the onion briskly without any oil in a heavy-based or non-stick frying pan until transparent. Roast the besan flour and ground cumin together, then remove them from the pan and roast the chirongi nuts, almonds and poppy seeds; grind these ingredients together.

Mince the meat to a fine paste with all the remaining ingredients apart from the egg and oil. Mix the egg thoroughly into the meat paste, then make small sausage shapes from the mixture. These should be fixed on to skewers and (ideally) they should be cooked over charcoal. Alternatively, lightly brush the kabaabs with oil and cook them under a hot grill. Turn the kabaabs several times during cooking. Serve with a salad and thinly sliced onions. SERVES 4

Quick Fried Kabaabs

———— Kacheh Gosht Ke Kabaab ————

450 g/1 lb lean braising steak
salt
¼ teaspoon papaya pulp or meat tenderiser
(optional)
3 medium onions, finely chopped
1 small very firm tomato, finely chopped
2 tablespoons chopped fresh coriander leaves
1 tablespoon chopped mint
2 or 3 green chillies, chopped
1 clove garlic, crushed
1 teaspoon ground black pepper
1 egg
a little oil for frying
GARNISH
coriander sprigs

This dish takes about 45 minutes to prepare. Cut the meat into small pieces and mince it three times, or until it forms a fine paste. Mix with the salt and papaya or tenderiser and set aside. Mix all the remaining ingredients together, then knead them into the meat, making sure that they bind together.

Divide the mixture into six to eight portions and flatten them between the palms of your hands. Fry with as little oil as possible in a non-stick frying pan until they are crisp and brown on both sides, and cooked through. Serve immediately, sprinkled with a little lemon juice and garnished with coriander sprigs. SERVES 4

Spicy Slivers of Meat

Lamboorian

450 g/1 lb fillet steak
1 clove garlic, crushed
½ teaspoon ground ginger
¼ teaspoon turmeric
1 teaspoon chopped green chillies
1 teaspoon salt
oil for cooking
juice of 1 lemon
lemon wedges to garnish

This dish takes about 30 minutes to prepare. Cut the meat into fine strips. Mix the garlic, ginger, turmeric, green chillies and salt together, then smear evenly over the meat.

Heat a little oil in a non-stick frying pan, then cook the meat, a few strips at a time, until browned all over. The meat should be cooked quickly over a high heat. Serve immediately, sprinkled with the lemon juice and garnished with lemon wedges. SERVES 4

Note: This dish has no sauce or gravy, so serve it with a kari – for example you could try Renu's Favourite (*Dahi Ki Kari*) on page 73. Hyderabadi Dal (page 66) can also be served with this dish as illustrated above.

Fenugreek Tempered Tomato Beef

Tomate Methi Gosht

150 ml/¼ pint oil
1 teaspoon fenugreek seeds
1 teaspoon mustard seeds
12 curry leaves
2 medium onions, chopped
2½ teaspoons Standard Four Spices (page 12)
1½ teaspoons salt
450 g/1 lb lean braising steak, diced
300 ml/½ pint water
1 kg/2 lb tomatoes, chopped

This dish takes about 2 hours to prepare. Heat the oil, add the fenugreek and mustard seeds together with eight of the curry leaves. Cover the pan and allow to cool for 2 minutes.

Add the onions, Standard Four Spices and salt and cook, stirring continuously, for about 2 minutes. Then add the meat, remaining curry leaves and water. Cook, covered, until the water begins to boil, then lower the heat and simmer gently until the meat is tender – about 1½ hours. Now add the chopped tomatoes and cook briskly without the lid to reduce the liquid until it makes a thick sauce. Cover the pan and leave over a very low heat for 5 to 10 minutes. Serve hot. SERVES 4

Note: The cooked dish should have a strong aroma of fenugreek and a thin layer of oil on the surface.

Samosa Mince

―――― *Samoseh Ka Kheema* ――――

(Illustrated on pages 6 and 7)

8 medium onions, chopped
6 green chillies, chopped
450 g/1 lb beef, finely minced
1 teaspoon salt
¼ teaspoon pepper
2 tablespoons oil (if necessary)
onion rings to garnish

This dish takes about 25 minutes to prepare. Mix the chopped onions and chillies into the meat, season with the salt and pepper and place in a heavy-based saucepan or large frying pan with a lid. Cover and cook for about 20 minutes.

Remove the lid and continue cooking until all the liquid has evaporated. Continue to fry, stirring continuously and adding the oil if necessary, until the meat is lightly browned and separated. Serve hot, garnished with onion rings. SERVES 4

Mince Tempered with Whole Spices

―――― *Baghara Kheema* ――――

(Illustrated on pages 6 and 7)

4 tablespoons oil
1 teaspoon cumin seeds
4 cloves garlic, sliced in half
8 curry leaves
4 dried red chillies
450 g/1 lb beef, finely ground
2 teaspoons salt
2 lemons

This dish takes about 30 minutes to prepare. This recipe starts off with a baghar: heat the oil in a heavy-based saucepan and add the cumin seeds, garlic, curry leaves and chillies. When the garlic is golden brown add the minced beef and salt. Cover the pan, lower the heat and cook for 20 minutes. Remove the lid and fry for a few more minutes, stirring all the time, until the mince is separated.

Cut the lemon into 3-mm/⅛-in slices, removing all the pips and skin. If the skin is not removed the mince will have a slightly bitter taste. Now add the slices to the mince and cover the pan, then leave over a very low heat for about 5 minutes. Serve immediately. SERVES 4

Ginger Kabaab

―――― *Sulaimani Kabaab* ――――

450 g/1 lb lean tender lamb (for example fillet)
juice of 1 lemon
1 teaspoon Standard Four Spices (page 12)
1½ teaspoons salt
2.5-cm/1-in piece fresh root ginger
225 g/8 oz pickling onions
2 tablespoons oil

This dish requires at least 1 hour's marinating time and 30 minutes' preparation. Cut 5-mm/¼-in slices across the grain of the lamb and marinate them in the lemon juice, Standard Four Spices and salt. Allow at least 1 hour for marinating the meat.

Slice the ginger very finely. Arrange alternate pieces of meat, pickling onions and slices of ginger on skewers. There should be enough for four people: four large skewers or eight small ones. Cook under a hot grill or over charcoal, basting the kabaabs frequently with the oil and turning them frequently until the meat is golden brown. Serve immediately. SERVES 4

Spiced Fried Kidneys

―――― *Taleh Hueh Gurdeh* ――――

8 lamb's kidneys
1 large clove garlic, crushed
½ teaspoon salt
2 tablespoons vinegar
large knob of butter
4 green chillies, finely chopped

This dish takes about 30 minutes to prepare. Halve and core the kidneys and rinse them under cold running water. Mix the kidneys with the garlic, salt and vinegar.

Melt the butter in a heavy-based saucepan with a close-fitting lid. Add the kidneys and cook, stirring until they are well browned. Cover the pan and cook over a low heat for 5 minutes. Remove the lid and continue cooking, stirring, until the juices have evaporated. Sprinkle the finely chopped green chillies over the kidneys and serve. SERVES 4

Clockwise from the top left: Ganwar Beans (page 63), garnished with red chilli tassels, Spiced Fried Kidneys, Ginger Kabaab and Sliced Aubergines in Yogurt (page 80)

Double Onion Beef

—————— *Nimboo Ka Do Pyaza* ——————

6 tablespoons oil
450 g/1 lb lean frying steak, cut into
1.5-cm/$\frac{3}{4}$-in cubes
6 medium onions, finely chopped
2$\frac{1}{2}$ teaspoons Standard Four Spices (page 12)
1$\frac{1}{2}$ teaspoons salt
2 lemons *or* 100 g/4 oz gooseberries
8 curry leaves
2 green chillies, chopped

This dish takes about 2$\frac{1}{4}$ hours to prepare. Heat the oil in a heavy-based saucepan and cook the meat, onions, Standard Four Spices and salt, covered, for about 45 minutes, or until the meat is tender. Meanwhile simmer the lemons (if used) in water to cover for 5 minutes, or until they are soft.

When the meat is tender, the onions should be pink and most of their liquid should have evaporated. Remove the lid from the pan and cook quickly to evaporate any liquid which remains, then fry, stirring continuously, until the meat and onions are lightly browned. Add the gooseberries at this stage if they are being used. Cut the ends off the lemons and chop the rest finely, removing the pips. Add the lemons to the meat, with all their juice and the curry leaves. Cover and cook over a gentle heat until the oil surfaces. Add the chillies and continue cooking for a further 10 minutes. Serve hot. SERVES 4

Layered Baked Beef

—————— *Tas Kabaab* ——————

675 g/1$\frac{1}{2}$ lb lean chuck steak, thinly sliced
2 teaspoons salt
juice of 2 lemons
$\frac{1}{4}$ teaspoon saffron strands
3 tablespoons boiling water
8 medium onions, sliced
250 ml/8 fl oz oil
3 cloves
2 (2.5-cm/1-in) pieces cinnamon stick
1 teaspoon whole black pepper
4 cardamoms
4 green chillies
8 fresh coriander sprigs
4 mint sprigs

This dish requires 1 hour's marinating and about 1$\frac{1}{4}$ hours' preparation. Remove all the fat from the meat; the slices should be no more than 5 mm/$\frac{1}{4}$ in thick. Cut the slices into pieces — 5 × 7.5 cm/2 × 3 in. in size. Marinate the pieces of meat in the salt and lemon juice for about 1 hour.

Pound the saffron and mix the strands with the boiling water. Fry the onions in the oil; when they are transparent remove half of them from the pan and set aside. Continue frying the remaining onions until they are golden brown, then spread these on absorbent kitchen paper to remove the excess oil. Reserve the oil in the pan.

Pour half the reserved oil into an ovenproof casserole, then add the transparent onions, half the whole spices, the meat, browned onions, chillies, coriander and mint. Pour in the marinating juices from the meat and the remaining oil, then top with the rest of the whole spices and, finally, the saffron. Cook, covered, in a moderately hot oven (200c, 400F, gas 6) for about 1 hour or until the meat is tender. SERVES 4 TO 6

Baked Kabaab

Dum Ke Kabaab

3 medium onions, sliced
5 tablespoons oil
2 tablespoons poppy seeds
150 ml/$\frac{1}{4}$ pint natural yogurt
8 black peppercorns
3 cloves
$\frac{1}{2}$ teaspoon papaya pulp or meat tenderiser
(optional)
675 g/1$\frac{1}{2}$ lb lean chuck steak, thinly sliced
salt
$\frac{1}{4}$ teaspoon saffron strands
4 tablespoons boiling water

GARNISH
coriander sprigs
strips of carrot

This dish requires 1 hour's marinating time and about 2 hours' preparation. Fry the onions in the oil, then set them aside to drain on absorbent kitchen paper. Reserve the oil. Roast and grind the poppy seeds in a liquidiser with the onions, then mix with the yogurt. Add the peppercorns, cloves and papaya or meat tenderiser and blend thoroughly in a liquidiser. Cut the meat into 5-cm/ 2-in strips and marinate these in the yogurt mixture, adding salt to taste, for not less than 1 hour. Meanwhile, pound the saffron and mix it with the boiling water. Set aside.

Grease a baking dish. Arrange the meat and marinade in the dish, sprinkle the saffron solution and remaining oil over the meat and bake, covered, in a moderate oven (180C, 350F, gas 4) for 1$\frac{1}{2}$ hours. Serve, garnished with coriander sprigs and fine strips of carrot. SERVES 4 TO 6

Baked Spicy Mince

Dum Ka Kheema

2 tablespoons poppy seeds
2 cloves
8 peppercorns
2 medium onions, sliced
3 tablespoons oil
1 teaspoon chilli powder
150 ml/$\frac{1}{4}$ pint natural yogurt
450 g/1 lb lean beef, finely minced
1 teaspoon papaya pulp or meat tenderiser
(optional)
salt
pinch of saffron strands
3 tablespoons boiling water
GARNISH
lime slices
coriander sprigs

This dish requires 2 hours' marinating and about 1$\frac{1}{2}$ hours' preparation. Roast the poppy seeds and grind them with the cloves and peppercorns. Fry the onions in the oil until they are golden brown, then drain them on absorbent kitchen paper to remove the excess oil. Reserve some onions for garnish, then chop the remainder very finely. Mix the chopped onions, ground spices, chilli powder, yogurt, minced beef and tenderiser with salt to taste, then leave to marinate for at least 2 hours. Grease a baking tray and spread the mixture evenly over it.

Pound the saffron and mix it with the boiling water. Sprinkle the saffron and the oil used to fry the onions over the kabaab. Cover with cooking foil and bake in a moderate oven (190C, 375F, gas 5) for 45 minutes. Remove the foil and cook for a further 15 minutes. The surface should be dark and crisp. Serve, garnished with lime slices and coriander sprigs. SERVES 4

Masala Kabaab

———— Kache Kheeme Ke Kabaab ————

450 g/1 lb lean minced beef
½ teaspoon ground ginger
2 large cloves garlic, crushed
1 onion, finely chopped
1½ tablespoons ground cumin, roasted
2 green chillies, finely chopped
½ teaspoon ground black pepper
1 teaspoon salt
2 tablespoons oil
GARNISH
small tomato wedges
radish slices
coriander sprigs

This kabaab takes about 30 minutes to prepare. Mix all the ingredients together thoroughly except for the oil. Grease a roasting tin or grill pan and spread the meat mixture evenly in it to a thickness of 1 cm/½ in. Keep the meat well bound together and make sure that the edges are evenly thick if the tin is too large to fill completely. If the kabaab is too thin it will burn, and if it is any thicker than 1 cm/½ in it will be under cooked.

Brush the surface of the meat with oil and cook it under a hot grill for about 15 to 20 minutes, or until browned and cooked through. Cut the kabaab into portions and serve hot, garnished with tomato wedges, sliced radish and coriander sprigs. SERVES 4

Fenugreek Mince

———— Kheema Methi ————

6 tablespoons oil
1 medium onion, sliced
1½ teaspoons Standard Four Spices (page 12)
450 g/1 lb minced beef
1 teaspoon salt
1 large potato, cut into 1-cm/½-in cubes
4 tablespoons chopped fresh fenugreek leaves
300 ml/½ pint water
2 tablespoons Hara Masala (page 12)

This dish takes about 30 minutes to prepare. Heat the oil in a heavy-based saucepan, add the onion slices and fry them until they are very lightly browned, then add the Standard Four Spices. Continue to fry, stirring, for 1 or 2 minutes then add the mince and salt. Fry the meat, breaking it up as it cooks, until the mince is well separated. Stir in the potato, fenugreek and water, then bring to the boil.

Cover the pan and cook gently for 10 minutes. Reduce the heat to the lowest setting and cook the mince for a further 10 minutes. Serve hot, garnished with Hara Masala. This mild dish goes well with Plain Rice (page 84) and Hyderabadi Dal (page 66). SERVES 4

Kidneys in Coconut Sauce

————————— *Kubut* —————————

8 lambs' kidneys
6 tablespoons grated fresh coconut *or* 3 tablespoons
desiccated coconut
150 ml/¼ pint boiling water
2 medium onions, chopped
2 tablespoons oil
1½ teaspoons Standard Four Spices (page 12)
salt
chopped fresh coriander leaves to garnish

This dish takes about 30 minutes to prepare. Remove the
outer skins from the kidneys, then cut them into quarters
and remove their cores.

Roast the coconut very lightly, then transfer it to a
basin and pour in the boiling water. Leave to soak until the
liquid has a milky appearance. If you are using desiccated
coconut it should be left for a little longer than the fresh
variety. Pass the liquid through a fine sieve, pressing the
coconut with the back of a spoon to squeeze out the last
drop of coconut milk. You should have collected about
150 ml/¼ pint of coconut milk.

Fry the onions in the oil until transparent. Add the
Standard Four Spices and kidneys and fry together,
stirring all the time, until the smell of raw spices
disappears. Pour in the coconut milk and add salt to taste,
then mix gently with the kidneys and cover the pan.
Leave over a low heat for 10 minutes. Serve hot, garnished
with chopped fresh coriander. SERVES 4

Spring Onion Liver

————————— *Kaleji Khara Masala* —————————

large knob of butter
1-cm/½-in piece fresh root ginger, chopped
3 cloves garlic, chopped
450 g/1 lb lamb's liver, finely sliced ,
1 bunch spring onions, finely chopped
1 green pepper, deseeded and finely chopped
1 tablespoon chopped fresh coriander leaves
3 green chillies, finely chopped
2 medium tomatoes, chopped
1 teaspoon salt
¼ teaspoon ground black pepper
spring onion curls to garnish

This dish takes about 30 minutes to prepare. Melt the
butter in a non-stick frying pan. Add the chopped ginger
and garlic and fry until the uncooked aroma has
disappeared. Add the liver and continue to fry for about
2 minutes.

Sprinkle the spring onions, green pepper, chopped
coriander, chillies and tomatoes over the liver and season
with the salt and pepper. Continue frying until all the
tomato juices have evaporated. Serve immediately,
garnished with the spring onion curls. SERVES 4

53

Subtle Beef Kabaabs

———— *Phirki Ke Kabaab* ————

(Illustrated on page 99)

3 medium onions
150 ml/¼ pint oil
4 teaspoons poppy seeds
pinch of saffron strands
2 tablespoons boiling water
450 g/1 lb lean stewing beef
2 tablespoons natural yogurt
1 teaspoon papaya pulp or meat tenderiser
(optional)
salt
1 teaspoon Garam Masala (page 13)
GARNISH
mint sprigs
lime wedges

This dish takes about 1¼ hours to prepare. Slice two of the onions and fry them in the oil, then drain them on absorbent kitchen paper. Roast and grind the poppy seeds. Pound the saffron and mix it with the boiling water.

Cut off and discard any fat from the meat, then cut the lean into small pieces. Roughly chop the remaining onion so that the pieces are the right size for a food processor or mincer. Mix all the ingredients apart from the saffron (including the fried onions) and mince the mixture to a very fine paste.

Shape walnut-sized portions of the mixture into small round, flattened kabaabs. Using your finger make a small depression in the centre of each kabaab. Arrange the kabaabs carefully on an oiled baking tray. Brush the meat with oil and in each depression put ¼ teaspoon oil and a drop of the saffron liquid.

Cover with cooking foil and bake for 25 minutes in a moderately hot oven (200C, 400F, gas 6) until brown. After 25 minutes baking, the kabaabs can be put under a hot grill to brown and finish cooking. Serve hot, garnished with sprigs of fresh mint and wedges of fresh lime. SERVES 4

Garam Masala Mince

———— *Muglai Kheema* ————

2 tablespoons Hara Masala (page 12)
3 tablespoons natural yogurt
450 g/1 lb lean ground minced beef
1 medium onion, sliced
50 g/2 oz urud dal
4 tablespoons oil
1½ teaspoons Standard Four Spices (page 12)
2 cloves
4 cardamoms
2.5-cm/1-in piece cinnamon stick
1½ teaspoons salt
a little Hara Masala (page 12) to garnish

This dish takes about 30 minutes to prepare. Mix the Hara Masala with the yogurt and set aside. Place all the other ingredients except for the salt in a heavy-based saucepan. Add enough water to just cover the mixture, bring to the boil, cover the pan and cook over a medium heat for 20 minutes or until the dal are almost cooked.

Remove the lid from the pan, raise the heat slightly and cook, stirring continuously. Add the yogurt mixture and salt, and continue cooking. The mince should separate as it cooks, and it should be fried until the oil has surfaced. At this stage the dals should be slightly darker and translucent. Serve immediately, garnished with a little Hara Masala. SERVES 4

Note: In Hyderabad this dish is accompanied by Renu's Favourite (page 73).

Clockwise from the top: Plain Rice (page 84), garnished with shredded red cabbage, Deep-fried Bread (page 96), Spongy Fritters in Yogurt (page 79) and Garam Masala Mince

Vegetarian dishes

India has the largest vegetarian community in the world. Pulses are the most economic source of protein to all who live in India. For the many vegetarians they are, in some form or another, a constant feature of every meal. This may sound dull – but on the contrary, lentils lend themselves to every aspect of Hyderabadi cookery. If not as a dal, then they are ground to flour for a bread, or made into a thick spongy batter.

In this chapter, lentils are soaked and fried for snacks, soaked and ground for dosas, cooked with very little water to make a dry vegetable dish, ground or partially ground to make fritters or cooked with a lot of water to make dals. The salt is always added to lentil dishes at the last minute otherwise the pulses will stay hard.

Some vegetarian recipes can be cooked very quickly; for example little advance thought is required for egg dishes. The selection of egg recipes needs no special ingredients apart, of course, from a stock of spices. They are all quick, extremely tasty, light and often mild; once you've tried some of them you'll wonder what you ever saw in scrambled eggs!

In addition to all the dishes made from pulses and eggs, this chapter includes vegetable dishes. There are many vegetables which are not easily found outside India. *Ganwar*, *Soni* and *Saim* are just three types of bean which are native to the Hyderabad region of India. Yams and gourds are also popular and these can occasionally be found in specialist greengrocers. Okra, another Indian favourite, is widely available.

There's a simple guide to vegetable cookery; make sure the vegetables are very fresh, small, firm and tender – this ensures the optimum flavour. Then, wherever possible, leave the skins intact to add flavour and vitamins; after that just follow the recipes.

Clockwise from the top: Semolina Dosa, Cauliflower in Coconut Sauce, Tiger Chick Peas and Steamed Chick Peas (all recipes overleaf)

Cauliflower in Coconut Sauce

— Phool Gobi —

150 ml/¼ pint boiling water
3 tablespoons desiccated coconut
1 medium cauliflower · 1 medium onion, chopped
4 tablespoons oil
2 teaspoons Standard Four Spices (page 12)
salt · 6 curry leaves
3 green chillies, chopped

This dish takes about 30 minutes to prepare. Pour the boiling water over the desiccated coconut. Leave for a few minutes, then strain off and reserve the coconut milk and squeeze all the remaining milk out of the coconut. Cut the cauliflower into small florets. Trim the central stalk and chop it into fine pieces, then finely chop the leaves.

Fry the onion in the oil until transparent. Add the Standard Four Spices and salt to taste, and fry, stirring continuously, for 2 minutes. Add all the chopped pieces of cauliflower and sauté for a further 4 minutes. Pour in the coconut milk, curry leaves and chillies and cook over a very low heat for 15 minutes, until the oil floats and all the flavours have mingled. Serve hot. SERVES 4

Semolina Dosa

— Rawa Dosa —

100 g/4 oz semolina · 1 tablespoon plain flour
1 tablespoon natural yogurt
450 ml/¾ pint lukewarm water · 7 tablespoons oil
1 green chilli, finely chopped
¼ teaspoon cumin seeds
¼ teaspoon salt · 50 g/2 oz butter

This recipe requires 30 minutes' soaking time and about 45 minutes' preparation. Mix the semolina with the flour then gradually stir in the yogurt and water to give a creamy pouring mixture. Leave to rest for 30 minutes.

Heat 1 tablespoon of the oil in a small pan, then add the chopped chilli and cumin seeds. Cook gently until the chillies have wilted and darkened. Pour this mixture over the batter and mix gently without creating too many air bubbles, adding the salt. The batter should have a thin pouring consistency.

Heat the remaining oil and butter together in a small pan until the butter melts. Keep this to hand to cook the dosas. Grease the surface of a griddle or non-stick frying pan with a little of the oil and butter mixture. Pour a ladleful of the batter on to the outer edge of the griddle. Quickly spread this inwards in a spiral to give a smooth dosa measuring about 25 cm/10 in. in diameter. Draw any excess batter back off the griddle and clean the edges of the griddle with the edge of a knife.

Pour a little of the butter and oil mixture around the dosa and ease the edges away from the griddle. Cook until lightly browned underneath, turn and cook the second side. Repeat with the remaining batter, stirring the batter each time you cook a dosa because it settles out on standing. Serve the dosas immediately they are cooked, with Dosa Potatoes (page 60). MAKES ABOUT 10

Tiger Chick Peas

— Chole —

225 g/8 oz chick peas
2 tablespoons cumin seeds
300 ml/½ pint tamarind extract (page 16)
1 small onion, finely chopped
1 tablespoon tomato purée · 1 teaspoon sugar
2 teaspoons salt · freshly ground black pepper
4 tablespoons Hara Masala (page 12)

This dish requires overnight soaking, plus about 40 minutes' preparation. Soak the chick peas for at least 6 hours in cold water to cover, then drain and boil them in fresh water until tender – 30 to 40 minutes. Meanwhile roast and roughly crush the cumin seeds.

Thoroughly drain the chick peas and return them to the saucepan. While they are still steaming, add all the other ingredients, saving a little Hara Masala for garnish. Cover and leave the chick peas to absorb the aroma of the herbs and spices.

Serve cold, garnished with the reserved Hara Masala. SERVES 4

Steamed Chick Peas

— Choleh Malai —

225 g/8 oz chick peas · 2 tablespoons oil
½ teaspoon cumin seeds
¼ teaspoon fenugreek seeds
2 green chillies, cut in slivers
4 curry leaves, cut into slivers · salt and pepper
½ teaspoon mustard seeds
150 ml/¼ pint soured cream
beetroot slices, cut into shapes, to garnish

This recipe requires 6 hours' soaking time and about 45 minutes' preparation. Soak the chick peas in cold water to cover for about 6 hours. Drain, then grind them to a smooth, thick paste, adding a little water as it is needed. A liquidiser is best for this process.

Heat the oil in a saucepan, then add the cumin and fenugreek seeds, chillies and curry leaves. Cover the pan and leave it off the heat for 2 minutes before stirring in the chick pea paste. Add 1 teaspoon salt and pepper to taste.

Cut eight squares of cooking foil – about 25 cm/10 in – and oil them well. Holding the foil in the palm of your hand, pour a ladleful of the mixture into each square, fold up the sides to enclose the paste in an envelope-shape package. Screw all the corners together in a knob to seal in the mixture. Alternatively, you can use small square foil containers. Stack the packages in a steamer and cook over boiling water for 20 minutes. Keep the water boiling all the time and check that it does not evaporate completely. Take care to keep the base of each package flat in the steamer to avoid having any wrinkles in the steamed chick peas.

Towards the end of the cooking time roast the mustard seeds in a heavy-based pan. Carefully unwrap the foil, mix the mustard seeds with the soured cream and pour over the chick peas just before serving, garnished with beetroot shapes. SERVES 8

Zebra Potatoes

———— Baghareh Aloo ————

5 tablespoons oil
1 teaspoon cumin seeds
4 dried red chillies
8 curry leaves
4 cloves garlic, split lengthways
4 medium potatoes, finely sliced
1 teaspoon salt

This dish takes about 20 to 30 minutes to prepare. Heat the oil, then add the cumin seeds, chillies, curry leaves and garlic. Cook until the garlic turns golden, then add the sliced potatoes and salt and cover the pan. Continue to cook over a low heat, stirring carefully and shaking the pan from time to time.

The potatoes will cook in their own moisture and steam; however, if they are not finely sliced you may have to add a drop of water. Serve the dish when the potatoes are tender and slightly transparent. Serve hot. SERVES 4

Note: The title 'Zebra Potatoes' is a nickname given to this favourite family dish of hotly flavoured, finely sliced potatoes.

Potato Aureoles

———— Aloo Tomate ————

2 medium onions, finely sliced
5 tablespoons oil
2 large cloves garlic, crushed
$\frac{3}{4}$ teaspoon ground ginger
$\frac{1}{4}$ teaspoon turmeric
1 teaspoon chilli powder
450 g/1 lb new potatoes, halved
300 ml/$\frac{1}{2}$ pint water
675 g/1$\frac{1}{2}$ lb tomatoes, chopped
1$\frac{1}{2}$ teaspoons salt
12 curry leaves

This dish takes about 35 minutes to prepare. Fry the onions in the oil until transparent. Add the garlic, ginger, turmeric and chilli powder. Cook, stirring, for a few minutes or until the aroma of garlic has died down. Add the halved potatoes and continue cooking for 3 minutes, then add the water and simmer, covered, for about 10 minutes or until the potatoes are almost cooked.

Stir in the tomatoes, salt and curry leaves, then cook, uncovered, over a medium heat until the juices are reduced by half. Cover the pan and leave over a very low heat for a further 15 minutes. Serve immediately. SERVES 4

Dosa Potatoes

— Aloo Masala —

3 tablespoons oil
6 curry leaves
$\frac{1}{4}$ teaspoon mustard seeds
$\frac{1}{2}$ onion, finely chopped
2 green chillies, finely chopped
pinch of turmeric
2 medium potatoes
$\frac{1}{2}$ teaspoon salt

Allow 25 minutes for preparing this dish. Heat the oil in a small saucepan, add the curry leaves and mustard seeds, then cover and cool, off the heat, for a couple of minutes. Add the onion, chillies and turmeric and sauté for 5 minutes.

Meanwhile, dice the potatoes. Add them to the pan, toss in the salt and pour in just enough water to cover. Simmer gently until the potatoes are tender. This masala should be fairly dry and medium-hot to taste. SERVES 4

Spiced Turnips

— Shaljam Methi —

4 tablespoons oil
1 teaspoon ground cumin
2 cloves garlic, sliced lengthways
2 dried red chillies
1 teaspoon fenugreek seeds
6 curry leaves
6 small young turnips
pinch of turmeric
1 teaspoon salt

This dish takes about 30 minutes to prepare. Heat the oil in a heavy-based saucepan which has a close fitting lid. When the oil is hot, remove the pan from the heat and add the cumin, garlic, chillies, fenugreek seeds and curry leaves. Allow to cool for 2 to 3 minutes.

Peel and halve the turnips, then cut them into very fine slices. Season these slices with a pinch of turmeric and the salt, then add the turnips to the spices. Cook, covered, for 5 to 10 minutes, making sure that the vegetables do not stick to the bottom of the pan. Keep the pan covered and leave over a very low heat for a few minutes. No water is needed to tenderise the turnips. Serve hot. SERVES 4 TO 6

Note: Choose small young turnips for this dish – the large woody variety are too tough.

Aubergine Discs

——— Taleh Baigan ———

1 teaspoon turmeric
1 teaspoon chilli powder
1 teaspoon ground coriander
1 teaspoon salt
1–2 tablespoons lime juice
2 aubergines
4 tablespoons oil
coriander sprigs to garnish

This dish requires 1 hour's standing time and it takes about 20 minutes to prepare. Mix the spices and salt with the lime juice to form a thick paste. Cut the aubergines into 5-mm/¼-in thick slices. Smear the paste over the slices and set aside for 1 hour.

Heat the oil in a large non-stick frying pan. Arrange the aubergines in the pan in a single layer, cover the pan and cook over a very low heat for about 5 minutes. Turn the aubergine slices, re-cover the pan and continue to cook for a further 5 minutes or until well fried. Serve immediately, garnished with the coriander. SERVES 4

Stuffed Peppers

——— Moti Mirchi ———

double quantity Dosa Potatoes (opposite page)
4 medium green peppers
1 lemon, thinly sliced
salt
lemon wedges to garnish

This dish takes about 1¼ hours to prepare. Prepare the Dosa Potatoes according to the recipe instructions and set aside.

Wash the peppers and cut the tops off them; reserve these caps. Remove all the seeds and pith from inside then place a slice of lemon in the base of each pepper. Season with a little salt, then fill each pepper with some of the potato mixture. Top the stuffed peppers with lemon slices and replace the reserved caps.

Stand the peppers in an oiled ovenproof dish, cover with cooking foil or a lid and bake in a moderately hot oven (190c, 375f, gas 5) for about 40 minutes, or until the peppers are cooked. Serve hot, garnished with lemon wedges.

Note: Select evenly sized, well-balanced peppers for this dish so that they will stand neatly when they are stuffed. Alternatively, the potato stuffing can be used to fill hot chilli peppers as illustrated on page 65.

Okra in Yogurt Sauce

Bhendi Ka Khorma

350 g/12 oz okra · 8 tablespoons oil
3 medium onions, finely chopped
2 teaspoons ground coriander
2½ teaspoons Standard Four Spices (page 12)
1½ teaspoons salt · 250 ml/8 fl oz natural yogurt
300 ml/½ pint water · 2 green chillies, chopped
½ teaspoon Garam Masala (page 13)

This dish takes about 45 minutes to prepare. Wash, top and tail the okra, then cut them in half widthways. Heat the oil in a heavy-based saucepan and fry the okra for 2 minutes to seal them. Remove from the pan and set aside. Add the onions to the oil remaining in the pan and cook until golden. Using a slotted spoon, remove the onions from the pan and drain them on absorbent kitchen paper.

Add the coriander, Standard Four Spices and salt to the oil in the pan. Cook, stirring continuously, for 2 minutes. Now add the yogurt, a tablespoon at a time, and continue cooking, stirring, until the yogurt solids are well fried to a light golden colour. Slowly pour in the water and add the fried onions, stirring constantly until a thick gravy is formed. After 5 minutes add the okra, then stir in the chillies and Garam Masala and cover the pan. Leave over a very low heat for a few minutes before serving hot.
SERVES 4

Okra in Hyderabadi Sauce

Khatti Bhendi

450 g/1 lb okra · 6 tablespoons oil
2 medium onions, finely chopped
2 teaspoons Standard Four Spices (page 12)
1 teaspoon salt · 6 curry leaves
150 ml/¼ pint tamarind extract (page 16)
150 ml/¼ pint water · 2 green chillies, chopped
1 tablespoon chopped fresh coriander leaves

This dish takes about 40 minutes to prepare. Wash, top and tail the okra. Heat the oil in a medium-sized saucepan, add half the okra and fry for 2 minutes. Remove and cook the remaining okra. This light cooking seals the vegetables and they become bright green; remove the okra and set them aside leaving the oil in the pan.

Add the onions to the oil remaining in the pan. Fry until transparent, then stir in the Standard Four Spices and salt. Cook, stirring, for 2 to 3 minutes before adding the curry leaves, tamarind extract and water. Bring to the boil, then add the okra, chillies and chopped coriander.

Cover the pan and leave over a very low heat for 10 to 15 minutes, or until the okra is tender. Do not overcook the okra or the dish will be slimy. Serve immediately.
SERVES 4

Ganwar Beans

———— Ganwar Ki Phalli ————

450 g/1 lb ganwar beans
1 small onion, chopped
4 tablespoons oil
2 teaspoons Standard Four Spices (page 12)
1 large tomato, chopped
1 small green pepper, deseeded and chopped
300 ml/½ pint water
salt

This dish takes about 40 minutes to prepare. Wash, top and tail the beans, stringing them if necessary, then cut them into 1-cm/½-in pieces. Fry the onion in the oil until just soft, then add the Standard Four Spices and cook for a further 2 minutes.

Stir in the beans and cook for a few minutes, then add the chopped tomato and pepper and pour in the water. Cover and cook gently until the beans are tender – about 25 minutes.

At the end of the cooking time most of the water should have evaporated. Stir in salt to taste and serve hot. SERVES 4

Creamed Spiced Lentils

———— Baghare Channa ————

225 g/8 oz gram dal
900 ml/1½ pints water
2 tablespoons oil · ½ teaspoon mustard seeds
2 whole red chillies
3 cloves garlic, sliced · 1 teaspoon salt
3 green or red chillies, finely sliced into rings
300 ml/½ pint soured cream

This dish takes about 1 hour to prepare. Place the gram dal in a saucepan and add the water. Bring to the boil, reduce the heat and simmer for about 25 minutes or until the dal is tender. Drain and set aside.

Heat the oil in a medium-sized saucepan and add the mustard seeds, whole red chillies and sliced garlic. Cook until the garlic is well browned, then cover the pan, remove it from the heat and leave to cool for 2 minutes. Add the drained dal to the spices, return the pan to the heat and cook gently until the dal and spices are well mixed. Stir in the salt with most of the sliced chillies and set aside to cool completely.

When the lentils have cooled mix in three-quarters of the soured cream. Spoon the mixture into a serving dish, pour the remaining soured cream on top and garnish with the remaining chilli rings. Serve cold. SERVES 4 TO 6

Temptation Dal

———— Khatte Chane ————

(Illustrated on front cover)

350 g/12 oz channa dal
3 tablespoons Hara Masala (page 12)
1 small onion, finely chopped
juice of 2 lemons
¼ teaspoon freshly ground black pepper
1 teaspoon salt
½ teaspoon sugar

This dish takes about 30 minutes to prepare. Cook the dal in plenty of boiling water until they are tender but not disintegrated – about 15 to 20 minutes.

Reserve 2 tablespoons of the Hara Masala for garnish. Drain the dal, then while still steaming hot add the remaining 1 tablespoon of Hara Masala and all the remaining ingredients. Stir well and set aside to cool.

Chill the cooled dal before serving, garnished with the reserved Hara Masala. SERVES 4 TO 6

Tamarind Eggs

———— Khatteh Ande ————

4 hard-boiled eggs
2 medium onions, finely sliced
6 tablespoons oil
1½ teaspoons Standard Four Spices (page 12)
450 ml/¾ pint water
6 tablespoons tamarind extract (page 16)
1½ teaspoons salt
4 curry leaves
2 green chillies

This dish takes about 45 minutes to prepare. Gently prick the eggs all over with a fork and set them aside. Fry the onions in the oil until they are transparent. Add the Standard Four Spices and cook, stirring all the time, for a few minutes. Pour in the water and tamarind, add the salt and curry leaves, and boil for about 10 minutes or until the sauce is reduced to half its original quantity. Stir regularly to prevent the sauce from sticking to the pan.

Add the eggs and whole green chillies with their stalks. Cover the pan and leave over a very low heat for about 10 minutes. During this time the oil should surface. Serve hot. SERVES 4

Simple Okra

———— Saadi Bhendi ————

(Illustrated on page 81)

450 g/1 lb okra
4 tablespoons oil
1 medium onion, chopped
1 large clove garlic, crushed
½ teaspoon ground ginger
1 green chilli, chopped
¾ teaspoon salt
300 ml/½ pint water

This dish takes about 30 minutes to prepare. Wash and trim the okra. Heat the oil in a saucepan, add the okra and cook for 2 to 3 minutes, or until the okra becomes bright green. Remove the okra from the pan and set aside.

Add the onion to the oil remaining in the pan, then stir in the garlic, ginger, chopped chilli and salt. Cook until the smell of raw garlic disappears, then replace the okra in the pan and pour in the water. Bring to a simmer, cover the pan and cook gently until the okra is just tender – about 15 minutes. Do not overcook the okra or it will become slimy. Serve immediately. SERVES 4

Clockwise from the top: Gram Lentil Fritters (page 100), Yellow Lentil Rice (page 91), Stuffed Chilli Peppers (see note, page 61) and Tamarind Eggs

Midnight Dal

Saabit Masoor

350 g/12 oz masoor dal
600 ml/1 pint water
2 medium onions, sliced
4 tablespoons oil
3 green chillies, chopped
1 teaspoon salt
¼ teaspoon freshly ground black pepper
juice of 1 lemon
chopped fresh coriander leaves to garnish

This dish takes about 45 minutes to soak and prepare. Soak the dal in enough cold water to cover for 25 minutes. Drain the dal and place them in a medium-sized saucepan with the water. Bring to the boil, then simmer gently until tender. Drain and set aside.

Fry the onions in the oil in a frying pan until they are almost golden. Add the chillies, salt and pepper, and continue cooking gently, stirring, for 1 to 2 minutes. Add the cooked lentils and cook, stirring continuously, until they are well mixed with all the other ingredients. Pour the juice of the lemon over the lentils and serve hot, sprinkled with the coriander. SERVES 4 TO 6

Hyderabadi Dal

Khatti Dal

175 g/6 oz masoor dal
900 ml/1½ pints water
1½ teaspoons Standard Four Spices (page 12)
3 green chillies
12 curry leaves
300 ml/½ pint tamarind extract (page 16)
1 tablespoon tomato purée
2 teaspoons salt
4 tablespoons oil
1 teaspoon cumin seeds
4 dried red chillies
4 cloves garlic, halved

This dish takes about 40 minutes to prepare. Place the dals in a saucepan with the water, Standard Four Spices, whole green chillies and six curry leaves. Bring to the boil, then reduce the heat and simmer until the dals have broken up. Add a little extra water if the dal begins to get too dry. Pour in the tamarind extract, then stir in the tomato purée and salt and simmer for a further 15 minutes. Mash the cooked dal with a potato masher or blend the mixture briefly in a liquidiser (first remove the whole chillies and curry leaves) until smooth and creamy.

In a separate pan, heat the oil until it is very hot, then add the remaining curry leaves, cumin seeds, dried red chillies and garlic. As soon as the garlic is golden, pour the oil and whole spices over the dal and cover the pan straightaway. Leave for 1 minute, then serve hot. SERVES 4

Eggs in Yogurt Gravy

Andon Ka Khorma

3 medium onions, finely chopped
6 tablespoons oil
6 tablespoons natural yogurt
$\frac{1}{2}$ teaspoon black cumin seeds
1 teaspoon Standard Four Spices (page 12)
$1\frac{1}{2}$ teaspoons ground coriander
salt
6 hard-boiled eggs
450 ml/$\frac{3}{4}$ pint water
$\frac{1}{2}$ teaspoon Garam Masala (page 13)
1 tablespoon Hara Masala (page 12)

This dish takes about 30 minutes to prepare. Fry the onions in the oil until they are soft. Pour in the yogurt, then add the black cumin seeds, Standard Four Spices, ground coriander and salt. Cook, stirring continuously, until the liquid from the yogurt has evaporated. The mixture of milk solids and spices will then turn a golden brown.

Lightly prick each hard-boiled egg with a fork to make sure that the flavour of the spices penetrates them. Pour the water into the pan and add the eggs. Do not cover the pan. Gently cook the eggs until they are heated through, then continue to cook over a very low heat until the oil rises to surface. Sprinkle with Garam Masala and cook for a few minutes, then add the Hara Masala and cook for a further few minutes before serving. SERVES 3 TO 4

Note: This dish can be served with rice or bread, or it can be included as a side dish in a more substantial meal.

Tomato Poached Eggs

Ande Tomate

6 tablespoons oil
6 cloves garlic, halved lengthways
8 curry leaves
6 small green chillies
1.25 kg/$2\frac{1}{2}$ lb tomatoes, chopped
$1\frac{1}{2}$ teaspoons salt
4 eggs
coriander leaves to garnish

This dish takes about 20 minutes to prepare. Heat the oil in a frying pan. Add the garlic, then when it begins to brown add the curry leaves and chillies. Cover the pan and remove it from the heat. After 2 minutes add the chopped tomatoes and salt and cook briskly for about 10 minutes or until the tomatoes are reduced to half their original quantity.

When the tomatoes are cooked, reduce the heat and carefully crack the eggs into the pan without breaking the yolks. Cover the pan and cook gently for about 5 minutes or until the eggs are cooked to taste. Serve immediately, garnished with coriander. SERVES 4

Note: These eggs – poached in a hot and piquant, powerful garlic sauce – make a good snack. Alternatively, they can be served as a side dish.

Classic Hyderabadi Aubergines

———— Baghare Baigan ————

4 small firm aubergines with stalks
salt
1 tablespoon ground coriander
1 tablespoon ground cumin
1 tablespoon sesame seeds
1 teaspoon poppy seeds
1 teaspoon chirongi nuts
4 tablespoons desiccated coconut
oil for deep frying *plus* 150 ml/¼ pint oil
1 teaspoon cumin seeds
19 curry leaves
1 tablespoon unsalted peanuts
4 cloves garlic, crushed
1 teaspoon ground ginger
½ teaspoon turmeric
3 teaspoons chilli powder
300 ml/½ pint tamarind extract (page 16)

This dish takes about 45 minutes to prepare. Wash and dry the aubergines and carefully cut them in half lengthways so that each piece is topped by half of the stalk. Lay the aubergines on a board, flat side down. Using a sharp knife, cut each half into four away from the stalk: they should open out to form a pear-shaped fan, held together at the stalk end. Soak the aubergines in a bowl of cold water with 1 tablespoon of salt added to prevent them from discoloring.

Roast the ground coriander and cumin together. Roast and grind the sesame and poppy seeds with the chirongi nuts, coconut and peanuts.

Heat the oil for deep frying to 185c/370f. Fry the aubergines for 2 to 3 minutes to seal the cut surfaces, then drain them on absorbent kitchen paper and set aside. Heat the 150 ml/¼ pint oil in a saucepan or skillet which is large enough to contain the aubergines without having them overlapping. Add the cumin seeds and 7 curry leaves. Cover the pan, remove it from the heat and allow to cool for 2 to 3 minutes.

Now add the garlic, ginger, turmeric and chilli powder and cook, stirring continuously, for 2 to 3 minutes. Add the ground roasted nuts. Season to taste and add the fried aubergines to the pan, arranging them so that they do not overlap. Do not stir, but shake the pan occasionally.

Pour in the tamarind extract and add the remaining curry leaves. Shake the pan, then cook, covered, over a very gentle heat for 15 minutes, or until the oil surfaces. Serve hot or cold, but do not reheat this dish. SERVES 4

Tomato and Coriander Sauce

———— Tomate Ki Kari ————

100 g/4 oz channa dal
1 kg/2 lb firm young tomatoes, peeled and chopped
1 medium onion, chopped
1½ teaspoons Standard Four Spices (page 12)
4 green chillies, chopped
3 tablespoons Hara Masala (page 12)
600 ml/1 pint water
1½ teaspoons salt
4 tablespoons oil
1 teaspoon cumin seeds
4 cloves garlic, sliced lengthways
4 red chillies
6 curry leaves

This dish takes about 1 hour to prepare. Cook the channa dal in plenty of boiling water for 30 minutes or until tender. Drain and return the dal to the pan. Add the tomatoes, onion, Standard Four Spices, chopped green chillies, Hara Masala, and measured water. Stir in the salt and simmer, uncovered, for 30 minutes.

At the end of the cooking time remove the pan from the heat and cool slightly. Blend the mixture in a liquidiser and pass it through a fine sieve to remove the tomato seeds. Pour the purée into a saucepan and reheat it gently.

Heat the oil in a small frying pan, add the cumin seeds, garlic, whole red chillies and curry leaves. When the garlic turns brown pour this spice mixture over the kari. Cover the pan to contain the aroma and remove from heat. Leave for a few minutes then serve hot. SERVES 4

Clockwise from the top: Saffron and Almond Spongy Dessert (page 115), Classic Hyderabadi Aubergines, Tomato and Coriander Sauce and Lamb Pilaff (page 86)

Wheat Dosa

Gehun Dosa

225 g/8 oz chapati flour or wholewheat flour
250 ml/8 fl oz natural yogurt
300 ml/½ pint water
3 curry leaves
1 teaspoon finely chopped fresh root ginger
¼ teaspoon salt
7 tablespoons oil
2 green chillies, chopped
pinch of mustard seeds
50 g/2 oz butter
pinch of bicarbonate of soda

These dosas take about 1½ hours to prepare. Place the flour in a bowl, then gradually mix in the yogurt and water to make a smooth batter with a thin pouring consistency. Leave to stand for 30 minutes. Use a pair of scissors to cut the curry leaves into fine slivers. Add the ginger, curry leaves and salt to the batter and stir well.

Heat 1 tablespoon of the oil in a small saucepan. Add the chillies and mustard seeds to the oil, then cover the pan and set aside to cool for 2 minutes. The chillies should darken during this standing time. Add the mixture to the batter and mix well. Heat the remaining oil with the butter until the butter melts, then remove from the heat and set aside for cooking the dosas.

Heat a griddle or non-stick frying pan over a medium heat. Just as you are ready to cook the dosas stir the bicarbonate of soda into the batter. Lightly grease the surface of the griddle with a little of the oil and butter mixture, then pour a ladleful of the batter on to the griddle. Spread the batter quickly and evenly, working inwards in a spiral motion, to give a smooth dosa, measuring about 23-25 cm/9-10 in. in diameter. Draw back and remove any excess batter. Pour a little of the oil and butter around the edge of the dosa and gently ease the set edges off the griddle. Use the edge of a clean knife to gently scrape away any stray bits of batter. Cook until lightly browned underneath, then turn the dosa over and cook until browned on the second side. Continue cooking the batter in this way until it is all used.

Serve immediately with a vegetable dish, for example Dosa Potatoes (page 60), and a chutney – try Tomato Chutney (page 106). MAKES ABOUT 6

Plain Dosa

Sada Dosa

50 g/2 oz urud dal
175 g/6 oz basmati rice
lukewarm water
¼ teaspoon salt
6 tablespoons oil
50 g/2 oz butter

This recipe requires overnight soaking and about 30 to 45 minutes to prepare. Carefully clean and wash first the dal, then the rice. Leave each to soak separately, in enough cold water to cover, for 3 hours. Drain both.

Place the dal in a liquidiser and blend with enough water to form a smooth paste. Transfer to a bowl. Put the rice in the liquidiser and cover with 5 mm/¼ in of water, then blend to a gritty paste. Mix the ground lentils and rice with enough lukewarm water to make a thick pouring batter. Cover and leave to stand overnight in a warm place. The mixture will start to ferment and thicken slightly on standing. Mix extra water into the batter to give a thick pouring consistency and stir in the salt. Heat the oil with the butter until the butter melts.

Heat the griddle over a medium heat and grease it with some of the oil and butter. Pour a ladleful of the batter on to the outer edge of the griddle and, working quickly in a spiral motion, spread it evenly to give a smooth, round dosa. Draw back any excess batter and remove it from the griddle.

Pour a little of the oil mixture around the edges of the dosa and lift the sides slightly, then leave to cook until lightly browned underneath. Turn and cook the second side. Continue cooking the doas in this way until all the batter is used. Serve immediately. MAKES ABOUT 6

To make *Masala Dosa*, stuff the cooked dosas with Dosa Potatoes (page 60). Serve with Coconut Chutney (page 104).

Festive Dal

— *Tu War Ki Dal* —

oil for deep frying
1 small aubergine, diced
100 g/4 oz toor dal
2 teaspoons Standard Four Spices (page 12)
10 curry leaves
600 ml/1 pint water
3 tablespoons lemon juice
1 tablespoon tomato purée
1 teaspoon salt
4 tablespoons oil
½ teaspoon mustard seeds
8 fenugreek seeds

This dish takes about 1 hour to prepare. Heat the oil for deep frying to 185c/370F. Add the diced aubergine and cook until lightly browned, then drain on absorbent kitchen paper and set aside.

Wash and drain the dal. Place them in a saucepan with the Standard Four Spices and four curry leaves. Pour in the water and bring to the boil. Continue boiling until the dal is tender. Simmer gently for 5 minutes, then add the lemon juice, tomato purée and salt. Add the fried aubergines and cook for a further 5 minutes.

Heat the 4 tablespoons of oil in a small frying pan and, when hot, add the mustard and fenugreek seeds with the remaining curry leaves. Pour this mixture over the dal a few minutes before serving. Cover the pan for the remaining short cooking time to contain the aroma. Serve hot. SERVES 4

Spinach Dal

— *Palak Dal* —

2 medium onions
900 ml/1½ pints water
225 g/8 oz red lentils
¼ teaspoon ground ginger
1 teaspoon salt
5 cloves garlic
100 g/4 oz fresh spinach, chopped
4 tablespoons oil
3 tablespoons soured cream
¼ teaspoon finely chopped fresh root ginger
3 teaspoons Hara Masala (page 21)

This dish takes about 1 hour to prepare. Chop one of the onions and slice the other. Pour the water into a medium-sized saucepan, add the lentils, chopped onion, the ground ginger and salt. Crush a clove of garlic into the pan and bring to the boil, then simmer until the lentils begin to disintegrate. Add the spinach and continue cooking for a further 15 minutes, stirring occasionally. Remove the pan from the heat.

Slice the remaining cloves of garlic lengthways. Heat the oil in a small frying pan, add the sliced garlic and sliced onion. Fry until golden brown, then pour this mixture over the dal and cover the pan closely to contain the aroma. Leave for a few minutes.

Serve, while hot, in a covered dish, topped with the soured cream and sprinkled with the fresh root ginger and Hara Masala. SERVES 4

Weekday Dal

Mithi Dal

175 g/6 oz red lentils
2 medium onions
3 tablespoons oil
4 cloves garlic, slit lengthways
1½ teaspoons Standard Four Spices (page 12)
600 ml/1 pint water
1 teaspoon salt
knob of butter
2 tablespoons Hara Masala (page 12)

This dish takes about 45 minutes to prepare. Wash the lentils, rinse them and leave to soak in fresh water until you are ready to cook them. Chop one onion and set aside. Finely slice and fry the other onion in the oil with the garlic until golden. Put two-thirds of the fried onions and garlic in a small saucepan to be used later. Continue frying the remaining onions until they are a dark brown.

Add the drained lentils, the chopped onion and Standard Four Spices to the onions, then continue to fry, stirring continuously, for 5 minutes. Pour in the water, bring to the boil and simmer for 15 minutes or until the lentils are well broken. Mash with a potato masher or until creamy in consistency. Stir in the salt and remove the pan from the heat.

Melt the knob of butter in the pan with the partially fried onions, heat for a minute and pour over the top of the lentils. Garnish with Hara Masala before serving hot.
SERVES 4

Renu's Favourite

Dahi Ki Kari

5 cloves garlic
4 tablespoons besan (chick pea flour)
½ teaspoon ground ginger
¼ teaspoon chilli powder
¼ teaspoon turmeric
3 teaspoons ground roast cumin
600 ml/1 pint natural yogurt
1.15 litres/2 pints water
4 tablespoons chopped spring onion
2 green chillies · 14 curry leaves
1½ teaspoons salt
1 quantity Gram Lentil Fritters (page 100)
4 tablespoons oil
1 teaspoon cumin seeds · 4 red chillies

This dish takes about 1 hour to prepare. Crush one clove of garlic and slice the others lengthways. Mix the besan, crushed garlic, ground ginger, chilli powder, turmeric, roast and ground cumin and yogurt to make a paste. Stir in the water, then strain into a large saucepan and bring to the boil over a high heat, stirring occasionally. (If the mixture is cooked over a low heat, or if the pan is covered the yogurt solids separate out.) Don't let the liquid boil over – it will rise just before it boils.

Reduce the heat so that the liquid simmers, add the spring onion, green chillies and six curry leaves. Simmer, stirring occasionally, until the liquid is reduced by half. Stir in the salt and cook until reduced to the consistency of thin yogurt. Meanwhile, prepare the fritters. When the kari is ready, heat the oil, add the cumin seeds, sliced garlic, red chillies and remaining curry leaves. Immediately the garlic browns pour the mixture over the kari and cover the pan. Just before serving float the fritters in the kari. Serve hot or cold. SERVES 4 TO 6

Raitas and salads

Although Zuju complains that her childhood food was bland and almost tasteless, her mother Baji gradually weakened over the years to her family's desire for spices in the food. However, the family food is still not as hot or spicy as in many other households. Hyderabadi friends vie for the chance to eat at 'Baji's Place'.

One of the attractions are the raitas and salads. Raitas are made from yogurt mixed with finely chopped or sliced vegetables such as cucumber or onion. Salads are not tradition-ally Indian, but they are healthy and usually consist of anything in season. Their dressings are light without oil – perhaps a little vinegar with cream and sugar, or quite simply the juice from fresh tomatoes seasoned with salt and pepper.

By preparing salads Zuju learnt how to chop fast and fine. On special occasions her Aunt would cut flowers out of the vegetables or create small animals out of mashed potatoes and three-quarters of an hour was nothing for the preparation of one salad.

Clockwise from top left: Black-eye Bean Salad, Beetroot and Soured Cream Salad and Mung Beans (all recipes overleaf)

Beetroot and Soured Cream Salad

— *Chugandar Raita* —

1 small cooked beetroot
3 tablespoons milk
150 ml/¼ pint soured cream
salt
freshly ground black pepper
¼ teaspoon mustard seeds, roasted

This raita takes about 10 minutes to prepare. Grate the beetroot and mix it with the milk, soured cream, salt and pepper. Chill lightly. Before serving sprinkle the roasted mustard seeds over the top of the salad. SERVES 4

Black-eye Bean Salad

— *Lobia* —

175 g/6 oz black-eye beans
1 clove garlic, peeled
½ small onion, finely chopped
salt
freshly ground black pepper
1 tablespoon chopped fresh dill
2 tablespoons olive oil
2 tablespoons vinegar
tomato slices to garnish

This salad requires overnight soaking and about 1 hour's preparation. Soak the beans overnight in plenty of cold water. Drain, then cook in plenty of unsalted boiling water until tender – about 45 to 60 minutes. Drain and set aside to cool slightly.

Smear a salad bowl with the garlic. Place the onion in the bowl with the beans, then add the remaining ingredients and toss well. Allow to cool completely before serving, garnished with tomato slices. SERVES 4

Mung Beans

— *Mung ki Dal* —

Sprouted mung beans are commonly associated with Chinese cuisine. If they are sprouted to no longer than 1 cm/½ in. in length they retain their full flavour and vitamin value (they are rich in Vitamin E).

Clean and wash the mung beans, carefully removing any grit or dirt. Lay them evenly on a deep plate and pour on just enough water to cover. Put the plate in a warm place: in the airing cupboard or near a boiler or radiator. Cover the plate to keep the light out and ensure that the beans stay white and tender as they grow.

Three or four days should be long enough to grow the sprouts. Twice a day top up the water to keep the mung beans covered. Thoroughly wash and dry the sprouts before use.

Serve the sprouted beans with a simple dressing or mix them into another salad. For example, they taste excellent when mixed with slices of avocado, dressed with a little oil, vinegar and seasoning to taste.

White Radish Salad

——— Mooli ———

1 large white radish, grated · salt
ground black pepper
2 tablespoons vinegar · ½ teaspoon sugar
1 tablespoon oil · 1 dried red chilli
pinch of mustard seeds
pinch of kalonji
pinch of cumin seeds
GARNISH
3 red radishes
a few white radish slices
a few curry or bay leaves

This dish takes about 15 minutes to prepare. Mix the radish with salt and pepper to taste, the vinegar and sugar. Heat the oil in a small pan, add the dried red chilli, mustard seeds, kalonji and cumin seeds. Cook gently for 1 to 2 minutes or until the cumin darkens slightly, then pour the mixture over the radish and set aside to cool.

For the garnish, cut down through the red radishes several times, leaving all the pieces attached at the base. Place the radishes in a bowl of ice cold water and set them aside for at least 30 minutes. Arrange the radish roses, slices of white radish and curry or bay leaves on the salad.

Red Cabbage Salad

——— Lal Gobi ———

½ small red cabbage
1 clove garlic, finely chopped
2 teaspoons sugar · 2 tablespoons vinegar
3 tablespoons olive oil · ½ teaspoon salt
freshly ground black pepper · 1 orange

This salad takes about 15 minutes to prepare. Cut the cabbage in half, then shred it finely, discarding the thick stalk as you do so. Place in a serving bowl. Crush the garlic in a small bowl with the sugar. Add the vinegar and stir until the sugar has dissolved. Then add the oil, salt and pepper; mix thoroughly. Pour this dressing over the cabbage and toss well. Chill lightly.

Grate and collect the rind off the orange. Halve the orange and squeeze out and collect the juice from one half. Remove the pips and skin from the other half and cut the flesh into thick slices. Halve these and reserve them for garnish.

Just before serving, remove the cabbage from the refrigerator – it will have become an intense pink in colour, releasing some of its own juice into the dressing – sprinkle in the orange rind and juice and toss well. Garnish with the halved orange slices and serve.
SERVES 4

Green Tomato and Sesame Salad

———— Hareh Tomateh va Til ————

3 green tomatoes
½ green pepper, deseeded and chopped
salt
freshly ground black pepper
1 tablespoon sesame seeds
strips of peel from 2 tomatoes to garnish

This dish takes about 15 minutes to prepare. Cut the tomatoes into eighths and mix them with the chopped green pepper, salt and pepper to taste.

Just before serving, roast the sesame seeds in a heavy-based, dry frying pan and sprinkle them over the salad. If the sesame seeds are sprinkled over the tomatoes too soon they become soggy and the salad loses its exciting crunch.
SERVES 4

Spicy French Beans

———— Phulli ————

225 g/8 oz tender French beans
¼ teaspoon ground ginger
1 small clove garlic, crushed
1 tablespoon oil
150 ml/¼ pint water
½ teaspoon salt
1 teaspoon chopped fresh mint
strips of peel from 2 tomatoes to garnish

This dish takes about 30 minutes to prepare. Wash, top and tail the beans, then cut them into 1-cm/½-in pieces. Fry the ginger and garlic in the oil for 1 minute, but do not let the garlic brown. Add the beans and continue to cook for 3 minutes, then pour in the water and salt and cook, covered, for 10 minutes. By the end of this cooking time the water should have evaporated. Stir in the mint and serve hot or cold, garnished with the strips of tomato peel arranged into roses. SERVES 4

Spongy Fritters in Yogurt

— Dahi Bare —

100 g/4 oz lentils
salt
pinch of baking powder
oil for deep frying
300 ml/½ pint thick-set natural yogurt
1-cm/½-in piece fresh root ginger,
peeled and chopped

This dish requires 3 hours' soaking time and 20 minutes' preparation. Wash and soak the lentils in cold water to cover for 3 hours. Blend the drained lentils in a liquidiser, adding just enough water to produce a smooth paste. Stir in a 1 teaspoon salt and the baking powder and mix thoroughly. Let the mixture rest for 5 to 10 minutes.

Heat the oil for deep frying to 185c/370f. Carefully drop a spoonful (just less than a tablespoon) of the mixture into the pan and fry until crisp on both sides. Continue until all the mixture is used. The fritters should be flat: if they are too rounded, or uncooked in the centre, thin the paste with 2 to 3 tablespoons water. Drain the cooked fritters on absorbent kitchen paper.

Mix the yogurt with an equal volume of water and pour the mixture through a fine sieve to ensure a smooth texture. Stir in ¾ teaspoon salt. Immerse the fritters in the yogurt, then leave for 20 minutes so that they swell and become spongy and soft. Chill, then serve topped with the chopped ginger. SERVES 6

Note: This mild raita makes an excellent accompaniment for most Indian dishes.

Rice Salad

— Buthi —

100 g/4 oz basmati rice
150 ml/¼ pint natural yogurt
3 tablespoons Hara Masala (page 12)
¼ teaspoon salt
freshly ground black pepper

This dish takes about 30 minutes to prepare, but the rice has to be cooled. Cook the rice according to the instructions given for Plain Rice (page 84), then drain it thoroughly and leave until cold.

Mix the cold rice with all the remaining ingredients and chill for at least 1 hour before serving. SERVES 2 TO 4

Note: You can make the garnish for this dish as elaborate as you like. Try making one or more roses from the thinly peeled skin of a tomato. Add fresh coriander leaves to complete the flower.

Avocado Coriander

———— Avocado Kothmir ————

2 avocado pears
2 tablespoons chopped fresh coriander leaves
4 tablespoons green olive oil
2 teaspoons clear honey
½ teaspoon salt
½ teaspoon ground black pepper
3 tablespoons white wine vinegar

This dish takes 5 minutes to prepare. Choose ripe avocados – those which feel hard are not ripe. Mix the chopped coriander, oil, honey, salt, pepper and vinegar. Shortly before serving, halve the avocados and remove their stones. Pour the dressing into the cavity left by the stones and serve immediately. SERVES 4

Cucumber and Yogurt Raita

———— Dahi Ka Raita ————

½ cucumber
300 ml/½ pint natural yogurt
½ teaspoon salt
freshly ground black pepper
a little chopped mint

This raita can be prepared in 10 minutes. Choose a fresh young cucumber. If young cucumbers are not available, peel strips of the skin off the side of older ones. Grate the cucumber and mix it with the yogurt, salt and pepper to taste. Chill and serve topped with chopped mint. SERVES 4

Sliced Aubergines in Yogurt

———— Dahi Baigan ————

(Illustrated on page 49)

300 ml/½ pint thick-set natural yogurt
300 ml/½ pint water
salt
freshly ground pepper
oil for deep frying
1 medium aubergine, thinly sliced

This dish takes about 40 minutes to prepare. Pour the yogurt through a fine sieve and mix it with the water in a bowl. Add salt and pepper to taste.

Heat the oil for deep frying to 185c/370F. Add the aubergine slices and fry them until they are lightly browned. Drain on a slotted spoon, then put the hot aubergines straight into the yogurt. Allow to cool for 30 minutes before serving. SERVES 4

Clockwise from the top: Coriander Rice (page 90), Cucumber and Yogurt Raita, Pistachio Ice Cream (page 118) scooped into a glass dish, Avocado Coriander, Simple Okra (page 64) and Chicken Hara Masala (page 34) with Creme de Menthe Drink (page 120)

Rice dishes

There is a simple rule of (finger and) thumb employed to test when the rice is cooked. After certain preparatory stages the rice is put into boiling water, then – at various stages of cooking – a few grains are removed and pressed between the finger and thumb. When the rice is uncooked each grain breaks into four pieces, when three-quarters cooked it breaks into three pieces. Half cooked and the grains break into two. When the rice is ready *the grains are still firm* but they squash evenly, between the finger and thumb.

Before Zuju arrived in Iran, this was about all she knew of rice cookery. One day she asked her daughter's nanny to check the rice which was cooking. The Iranian woman tasted the rice and spat it out in disgust. So humble Zuju observed while Pari cooked the rice.

She measured the rice into a large saucepanful of water. Very gently she washed the rice, taking great care not to break or crack the grains. The cloudy water was changed repeatedly until no more starch washed out. Pari then covered the rice with an inch of cold fresh water, threw in plenty of salt and soaked it for three hours. The rice was delicately scooped into a saucepan of boiling salted water, then she reduced the heat to simmer the rice; cooking was timed from this point, and it took 5 to 6 minutes.

The rice was then drained, keeping one cupful of the liquid. Oil was then poured into another large saucepan and, using a flat spoon, the rice was layered into the pan in the shape of a cone. Using the handle of a wooden spoon, Pari now made one central hole in the cone and two or three others into the side of the rice at a slight angle to the centre. The cup of liquid was poured into the holes, the pan was covered with a thick towel and the lid was jammed firmly on top. The saucepan was set on the stove over a moderate heat. After five minutes the heat was turned to its lowest and the rice left to continue cooking for an hour.

Zuju was convinced that this was the best way to cook rice. For day to day cooking she has telescoped the above method into a simple recipe.

Clockwise from the top: Gram Soured Rice, Plain Rice (both overleaf), Cabbage Rice and Coriander Rice (both page 90)

Gram Soured Rice

— Channe Ki Khubooli —

350 g/12 oz basmati rice
salt
$\frac{1}{4}$ teaspoon saffron strands
4 tablespoons boiling water
100 g/4 oz channa dal
2 medium onions, sliced
5 tablespoons oil
$\frac{1}{2}$ teaspoon ground ginger
1 clove garlic, crushed
150 ml/$\frac{1}{4}$ pint natural yogurt
1 teaspoon black cumin seeds
2.25 litres/4 pints water
3 green chillies, chopped
1 tablespoon chopped fresh coriander leaves
1$\frac{1}{2}$ teaspoons chopped mint
1 teaspoon Garam Masala (page 13)
grated rind and juice of 2 lemons

This dish takes about 1$\frac{1}{2}$ hours to prepare. Wash the rice and soak it in cold water, with 3 teaspoons salt added, for 20 minutes. Meanwhile pound the saffron, add the 4 tablespoons boiling water and set aside. Clean and wash the dal and cook in plenty of boiling unsalted water for 20 to 25 minutes until tender but still firm. The dal should not be overcooked at this stage or they will disintegrate later. Drain off all the water.

Fry the onions in 2 tablespoons of the oil until golden brown. Drain on absorbent kitchen paper and set aside. In the same oil, fry the ginger and garlic, stirring continuously, for 2 minutes. Add 1 tablespoon yogurt and continue cooking, stirring, until all the liquid has evaporated and the yogurt solids are light gold in colour. Continue cooking in this way, gradually adding the yogurt in small quantities at a time, until all the yogurt solids are cooked.

Bring the water to the boil in a large saucepan (one which will hold up to 2.25 litres/5 pints of water). Add the black cumin, 3 teaspoons salt and the rice, then simmer until the rice is almost cooked – about 4 minutes. Remember to check the rice during cooking by squeezing the grains between your finger and thumb. Drain the rice, reserving 50 ml/2 fl oz of the cooking water. Mix the green chillies, chopped coriander and mint to make Hara Masala.

Pile the ingredients into a cone shape in a large saucepan, layering them as follows:

1	2 tablespoons oil	7	prepared Hara Masala
2	one-third saffron liquid	8	remaining Garam Masala
3	one-third rice	9	half onions
4	half Garam Masala	10	remaining rice
5	dal	11	remaining onions
6	second third of rice	12	remaining 1 tablespoon oil

Using a wooden spoon handle, and taking great care, make a hole down the middle of the cone of rice. Make two or three other holes at an angle into the side of the cone. Sprinkle the reserved rice water, lemon rind and juice, remaining saffron liquid and yogurt over the cone.

Cover the saucepan with a double thickness of tea towel and place a close-fitting lid on top. Fold the sides of the tea towel over the top of the lid so that they do not burn during cooking. Cook the rice for 5 minutes over a medium heat, then reduce the heat and cook very gently for 10 to 15 minutes. Gently mix the rice, lentils and onions just before serving. Serve hot. SERVES 6

Plain Rice

— Khushka —

225 g/8 oz basmati rice
1.4 litres/2$\frac{1}{2}$ pints water
1$\frac{1}{2}$ teaspoons salt

Rice takes about 25 minutes to prepare. It is essential to wash basmati rice first if you want to be sure that the grains will cook separately. Put the rice in a bowl and add plenty of tepid water. Gently swirl the water with your hand – it will become cloudy as the starch washes out of the rice. Change the water and continue washing. Keep changing the water until there is no more starch to wash out and the water is clear. Take great care not to damage the grains of rice.

Pour not less than 1.4 litres/2$\frac{1}{2}$ pints cold water into a large saucepan. Add the salt and the rice. Bring the water to the boil, then simmer, uncovered, until the grains are tender. From the time you put the rice in the water and turn on the heat, the grains will take 20 minutes to cook. If you allow 20 minutes from the time the water comes to the boil you will end up with a soggy mess best used for wallpaper paste!

To cook properly, rice needs as much space as possible; if a larger saucepan is used more water can be added. Throughout cooking – perhaps every 4 to 5 minutes – the rice should be tasted to see how tender it is.

When the rice is cooked, drain off all the water. Return the rice to the saucepan, cover the pan and leave the rice for about 5 minutes before serving. It will be just right at the end of this standing time. The cooked rice can be garnished with a variety of ingredients – like chopped chillies, spring onions or beetroot, or ground roast cumin and paprika. SERVES 4

Vegetable Pilaff

— *Tarkari Pulao* —

175 g/6 oz basmati rice
¼ teaspoon saffron strands
4 tablespoons boiling water · 2 medium onions
50 g/2 oz butter · oil for deep frying
1 small potato, diced · 50 g/2 oz peas
¼ small cauliflower, broken into florets
100 g/4 oz cut French beans
1 medium carrot, diced · salt
½ teaspoon black cumin seeds
½ teaspoon ground ginger
1 clove garlic, crushed
3 green chillies, sliced
1 teaspoon Garam Masala (page 13)

This dish requires soaking for 20 minutes and about 1 hour for preparation. Wash the rice, then soak it in enough fresh water to cover for 20 minutes. Pound the saffron and mix it with the boiling water; set aside. Fry the onions in the butter until golden brown, then drain them on absorbent kitchen paper. Keep the butter. Heat the oil for deep frying to 185 c/370 f. Fry the vegetables for 2 minutes, then lay them out on absorbent kitchen paper and sprinkle with 1 teaspoon salt.

Bring at least 3 litres/5 pints water to the boil. Add 3 teaspoons salt and the black cumin seeds. Drain the rice and add it to the water. Bring back to the boil, then reduce the heat and simmer for 4 to 5 minutes, or until the rice is three-quarters cooked. Drain the rice and save 50 ml/2 fl oz of the cooking water.

In a large saucepan, heat the butter used for cooking the onions. Add the ginger and garlic and fry, stirring continuously, for 2 minutes. Remove the pan from the heat, add the reserved rice water and arrange the remaining ingredients in layers to form a cone as follows:

1 half rice
2 fried vegetables
3 green chillies
4 fried onions
5 remaining rice
6 Garam Masala
7 saffron liquid

Cover the pan with one or two tea towels and place a tight-fitting lid on top. Fold the cloth over the top of the lid to prevent the edges from burning, then cook over a moderate heat for 4 to 5 minutes. Reduce the heat to its lowest setting and cook very gently for about 15 to 20 minutes.

Before serving, carefully mix all the vegetables with the rice. Serve hot. SERVES 4

Lamb Pilaff

— *Pulao* —

450 g/1 lb lean tender lamb (cut from the leg)
1½ teaspoons ground ginger
5 cloves garlic, crushed
300 ml/½ pint natural yogurt
225 g/8 oz basmati rice
salt · ½ teaspoon saffron strands
450 ml/¾ pint boiling water · 4 green chillies
2 tablespoons chopped fresh coriander leaves
1 tablespoon chopped mint
5 medium onions, finely sliced · 4 tablespoons oil
small piece of mace (about the size of a fingernail)
1 teaspoon black cumin seeds
2.5-cm/1-in piece cinnamon stick · 4 cardamoms
2 cloves · 40 g/1½ oz butter
2 teaspoons Hara Masala (page 13) · 50 ml/2 fl oz milk
grated rind and juice of 1 lemon
hard-boiled eggs to garnish

This dish needs 2 hours' marinating and about 1½ hour's preparation. Remove any surplus fat from the lamb and cut the lean part into small pieces. Mix the ginger and garlic with the yogurt and marinate the meat in this mixture for 2 hours. Thoroughly wash the rice and soak it in enough cold water to cover, with 3 teaspoons salt, for 2 hours.

Before you continue to the next stage make sure that all the ingredients are conveniently close to hand. Pound the saffron strands and mix them with 150 ml/¼ pint of the boiling water. Mix the whole green chillies with the chopped coriander and mint to make Hara Masala.

In a large, heavy-based saucepan, fry the onions in the oil until they are golden brown. Set aside on absorbent kitchen paper to drain. Add the meat with its marinade and 1 teaspoon salt to the oil remaining in the pan. Cook for 5 to 10 minutes, or until the pieces of meat are sealed, and the yogurt solids are lightly browned. Now add the remaining 300 ml/½ pint boiling water, cover the pan and cook over a moderate heat until the meat is almost cooked – 20 minutes for tender young lamb, or up to 45 minutes for a slightly tougher joint. Meanwhile, grind half the onions with the mace and add this to the meat. Leave the meat over a very low heat until the rice has soaked.

While the meat is cooking, drain the rice. Add 3 teaspoons salt to at least 3 litres/5 pints water and bring it to the boil. Add the black cumin seeds, cinnamon stick, cardamoms, and rice, then bring back to the boil. Reduce the heat and simmer for no more than 3 minutes. Drain the rice.

You must now work quickly to make a cone of all the ingredients in a large saucepan, taking care that the rice does not cool off. First melt the butter in the saucepan, then arrange the ingredients into a cone shape as follows:

1	half saffron	6	Hara Masala
2	half rice	7	remaining rice
3	1 teaspoon garam masala	8	1 teaspoon Garam Masala
4	lamb (without its cooking juices)	9	remaining onions
5	half onions	10	1 teaspoon salt

Using the handle of a wooden spoon, make a hole down the middle of the cone and one or two other holes into the sides. Carefully pour the milk, meat juices, lemon rind and juice and remaining saffron liquid down the holes and over the cone.

Cover the pan with one or two tea towels and a tight-fitting lid. Fold the sides of the tea towels up on to the lid so that they don't burn during cooking. Cook over a very low heat for about 45 minutes. At the end of this time the pulao should be cooked. Gently mix the meat and rice together before serving hot, garnished with hard-boiled eggs. SERVES 4

Note: Pulao is served on elliptical platters (Mushqaab) especially on festive occasions such as weddings. The rice is decorated with a variety of fresh herbs and often hard-boiled eggs are added. The eggs are arranged round the edge of the platter. The rice should not be overcooked during the first stage of cooking or else it will become stodgy and sticky later. One method of avoiding this is to use generous quantities of ghee; however this makes the finished dish extremely rich.

Garam Masala Rice

— *Baghare Chaval* —

225 g/8 oz basmati rice
salt
1 medium onion, finely sliced
3 tablespoons oil
2 cloves
3 cardamoms
1-cm/½-in piece cinnamon stick
½ teaspoon black cumin seeds

This dish requires 30 minutes' soaking plus 30 minutes' preparation. Wash the rice in cold water, then soak it in fresh cold water to cover, with 3 teaspoons salt, for about 30 minutes.

In a large, heavy-based saucepan, fry the onion in the oil until golden brown. Using a slotted spoon, remove the onion from the pan and set aside to drain on absorbent kitchen paper. While the oil is still hot stir in the cloves, cardamoms, cinnamon stick and cumin seeds. Drain the rice, then add it to the spices with 1 teaspoon salt and the water. Bring to the boil, uncovered, then lay half the fried onions on top of the rice. Turn the heat down to its lowest setting, cover the pan and cook very gently for 15 minutes, or until all the water has been absorbed or evaporated and the rice is fluffy. Serve hot, garnished with the remaining fried onions. SERVES 4

Whole Lentils and Rice

—— Sabit Masoor Ki Khichri ——

175 g/6 oz basmati rice · salt
50 g/2 oz whole red lentils
¼ teaspoon saffron strands
3 tablespoons boiling water
2 medium onions, finely sliced · 4 tablespoons oil
1 teaspoon Garam Masala (page 13)
½ teaspoon black cumin seeds · 4 green chillies
4 tablespoons chopped fresh coriander leaves
1 tablespoon chopped mint

This dish requires up to 2 hours' soaking and 1¼ hours' preparation. Thoroughly wash the rice and soak it in fresh water, with 3 teaspoons salt, for at least 20 minutes. Wash the lentils and soak for 20 minutes in cold water without any salt. Pound the saffron and mix it with the boiling water; set aside. Fry the sliced onions in the oil and, when golden brown, drain them on absorbent kitchen paper. Keep the oil in which the onions were cooked. Mix the Garam Masala with ½ teaspoon salt.

Bring at least 3 litres/5 pints water to the boil. Add 3 teaspoons salt, the black cumin seeds, 2 whole green chillies and the rice. Bring back to the boil, then simmer gently until the rice is half cooked – about 3 minutes.

Drain the rice, which should be firm, and save 150 ml/ ¼ pint of the cooking water.

While the rice is cooking, boil 2 pints of water in another saucepan and add the lentils. Cook for about 10 minutes without salt. Drain off the water and sprinkle ½ teaspoon salt over the lentils. As soon as the rice and lentils are cooked work quickly so that they do not cool down. Layer all the ingredients into a cone shape in a large saucepan as follows:

1	two-thirds oil	7	remaining chillies
2	half rice	8	lentils
3	half Garam Masala	9	remaining onions
4	half onion	10	1 tablespoon saffron liquid
5	chopped coriander	11	remaining rice
6	mint	12	remaining Garam Masala

Make a hole down through the middle of the cone and two more into the sides (use a wooden spoon handle for this) then pour over the reserved rice water, remaining oil and saffron liquid. Cover first with one or two tea towels, then a tight-fitting lid and cook over a medium heat for 5 to 7 minutes. Lower the heat to a minimum and cook for 20 minutes.

To serve, mix all the ingredients and serve hot.
SERVES 4

Orange Rice

— Naranji Chaval —

225 g/8 oz basmati rice
salt
2 oranges
$\frac{1}{4}$ teaspoon saffron strands
4 tablespoons boiling water
2 medium onions, sliced
4 cloves
2 tablespoons oil
1 teaspoon black cumin seeds
grated rind and juice of 1 lemon
GARNISH
oranges slices
lemon slices

This dish requires 20 minutes for soaking and about 1 hour's preparation. Wash the rice and soak it in cold water to cover, with 3 teaspoons salt, for 20 minutes. Cut the oranges in half, squeeze out and collect the juice. Then remove all the pulp and save the skins. Place the orange skins in a small saucepan with enough water to cover. Bring to the boil, then simmer for 5 minutes. Drain and cool. When they are cool enough to handle remove all the white pith from the skins (use a teaspoon). Finely shred the peel and set aside. Pound the saffron and add the boiling water.

Fry the onions and cloves in the oil until the onions are golden. Remove the onions and drain them on absorbent kitchen paper, picking out all the cloves. Keep the oil.

Drain the rice and add this, with the black cumin seeds and 3 teaspoons salt, to at least 3 litres/5 pints boiling water. Bring back to the boil, then simmer for 4 to 5 minutes, until the rice is three-quarters cooked. Drain the rice and mix half of it with the saffron. Now arrange the rice and all the other ingredients in a large saucepan, layer by layer to make a cone shape as follows:

1 oil
2 plain rice
3 lemon rind
4 half onions
5 $\frac{1}{2}$ teaspoon salt
6 saffron rice
7 orange peel
8 remaining onions

Make a hole down through the middle of the cone. Make a further two holes into the sides of the cone – use the handle of a wooden spoon to do this. Sprinkle the lemon and orange juice over and add $\frac{1}{2}$ teaspoon salt.

Cover the pan with one or two tea towels and a tight-fitting lid. Fold the edges of the cloths over the lid and cook gently for 20 minutes. Mix the ingredients and serve hot, garnished with orange and lemon slices. SERVES 4

Coriander Rice

Hare Chaval

225 g/8 oz basmati rice · 25 g/1 oz butter
4 green chillies, finely chopped
1 bunch spring onions, finely chopped
salt · 1 teaspoon black cumin seeds
6 tablespoons chopped fresh coriander leaves
2 tablespoons chopped fresh mint
grated rind and juice of 1 lemon

GARNISH
strips of lemon rind
coriander sprigs

This dish needs 20 minutes for soaking and about 1 hour's preparation. Thoroughly wash the rice and soak it in enough fresh water to cover for 20 minutes. Melt the butter in a frying pan and fry the chopped chillies and spring onions until they have wilted. Remove from pan, but save the melted butter.

Bring at least 3 litres/5 pints water to the boil, then add 3 teaspoons salt, the black cumin seeds and rice. Bring back to the boil, then simmer for 4 to 6 minutes, or until the rice is three-quarters cooked. Drain the rice and reserve 50 ml/2 fl oz of the water.

Pour the reserved butter into a saucepan and arrange all the ingredients into a cone as follows:

1 one-third rice
2 coriander and mint
3 second third of rice
4 chillies and onions
5 remaining rice

Using the handle of a wooden spoon, make a hole down the centre of the cone and two others into the sides. Carefully pour the reserved rice water over and add the lemon rind and juice. Cover first with one or two tea towels, then a tight-fitting lid. Fold the edge of the cloth up on to the lid and cook over a moderate heat for 4 to 5 minutes. Continue to cook over the lowest heat setting possible for 30 minutes. Mix well and serve hot, garnished with the lemon rind, rolled up to form a rose shape, and coriander sprigs. SERVES 4

Cabbage Rice

Kullum

225 g/8 oz basmati rice · salt
1 medium onion, sliced · 5 tablespoons oil
1½ teaspoons Standard Four Spices (page 12)
3 green chillies, chopped
1 small cabbage, finely shredded
2 tablespooons water

This dish requires 20 minutes' soaking and about 1 hour's preparation. Wash the rice, then soak it in plenty of cold water with 1 tablespoon salt. Fry the onion in the oil until golden, then drain the slices on absorbent kitchen paper. Add the Standard Four Spices and chillies to the oil remaining in the pan, then fry these for 2 to 3 minutes. Stir in the cabbage and sauté for a few minutes, then add the 2 tablespoons water and salt to taste. Cover and cook gently for 15 minutes, then fry quickly until all the liquid has evaporated. Remove from the heat.

Drain the rice and cook it according to the instructions given in the recipe for Plain Rice (page 84). Drain the cooked rice.

Place the onions in the base of a large saucepan. Layer the rice and cabbage into a cone shape, starting with half the rice, then the cabbage and lastly the remaining rice. Cover the pan closely and leave over a very low heat for 10 minutes. Mix the ingredients and serve hot. SERVES 4

Spiced Potato Rice

— Tahari —

275 g/10 oz basmati rice
salt
1 medium onion, sliced
3 tablespoons oil
2 cloves garlic, crushed
$\frac{1}{2}$ teaspoon ground ginger
generous pinch of turmeric
2 medium potatoes, cut into 1.5-cm/$\frac{3}{4}$-in cubes
2.5-cm/1-in piece cinnamon stick
2 cloves
2 cardamoms
750 ml/1$\frac{1}{4}$ pints water
2 green chillies, chopped
chopped coriander to garnish

This dish takes about 1 hour to soak and prepare. Wash the rice and soak it for 20 minutes in cold water to cover, adding 3 teaspoons salt.

Fry the onion slices in the oil until golden brown; remove half of them from the pan and drain on absorbent kitchen paper. Add the garlic, ginger, turmeric and potatoes and cook, stirring, for 3 to 4 minutes. Now add the whole spices and carefully stir them off the base of the pan to prevent them from sticking.

Add the drained rice and 1 teaspoon salt, then pour in the water, cover the pan and bring to the boil. Lower the heat, gently turn the rice so that the bottom layer is at the top and add the chopped chillies. Cover and cook gently for 10 minutes or until the grains are cooked and the liquid has been absorbed. Serve hot, garnished with the reserved, fried onions and coriander. SERVES 4 TO 6

Yellow Lentil Rice

— Khichri —

175 g/6 oz basmati rice · 50 g/2 oz red lentils
salt · 1 medium onion, finely sliced
3 tablespoons oil · $\frac{1}{8}$ teaspoon turmeric
$\frac{1}{2}$ teaspoon ground ginger · 1 clove garlic, crushed
2 cloves · 2 cardamoms
1-cm/$\frac{1}{2}$-in piece cinnamon stick · 650 ml/22 fl oz water
2 tablespoons Hara Masala (page 12)

This dish requires 5 to 30 minutes' soaking time and about 30 minutes' preparation. Thoroughly wash the rice and lentils together. Soak both in enough cold water to cover, with 3 teaspoons salt, for at least 5 minutes. In a large, heavy-based saucepan, fry the finely sliced onions in the oil until golden brown, then set aside on absorbent kitchen paper to drain. Add 1$\frac{1}{2}$ teaspoons salt, the turmeric, ginger and garlic to the oil remaining in the pan. Stir in the cloves, cardamoms and cinnamon stick and cook, stirring all the time, for 2 to 3 minutes.

Throughly drain the rice and lentils (any extra water will hinder the cooking) then add them to the pan and continue to fry, stirring, for a further 5 minutes. Stir carefully with a flat wooden spatula, taking care not to break or crush the grains of rice. Pour the water into the pan and bring to the boil, then add most of the fried onions, leaving a few for the garnish. Immediately the water has started to bubble, stir gently to ensure that the contents of the pan are well mixed. Lower the heat, cover the pan and cook very gently for about 15 minutes, or until the rice and lentils are cooked. Sprinkle the Hara Masala over the rice and leave over a very low heat for another 2 to 3 minutes. Serve hot, garnished with the reserved fried onions. SERVES 4

91

Breads and snacks

In the following recipes for different Indian breads, guidelines can be given for the preparation times. However, the actual rolling out of the dough will largely depend on the cook's experience. Again, the cooking times for different breads are never too long, but they will depend on the equipment and experience.

Although a good cast iron frying pan can be used for cooking bread, for a very small investment a *tawa* can be bought from a good Indian grocer. This is a slightly hollowed cast iron pan. The hollow centre collects the heat and it is perfect for cooking breads. In this chapter, a mixture of oil and butter are used to replace the more traditional ghee, which is expensive and extremely rich.

Indian breads are made from simple doughs of flour and water and require much more kneading than a European-style dough. This breaks down the gluten in the flour and changes the mixture from an unmanageable elastic mass to a dough which can be rolled into fine thin discs. Depending on the bread, doughs can be either firm or soft. Once the dough has been made, the usual procedure is to shape it into small balls between the palms of the hands. These are then flattened into small thick discs prior to rolling out. These discs are called *peras*. Most of the doughs are dusted with flour before cooking.

Some breads keep well but others dry out quickly. *Parathas* and *Rogni Roti* will keep for some time, especially the latter, but *chapattis* and *phulkas* do not keep.

From the top: Puffed Bread, Picnic Bread (both overleaf) and Fried Pasties (page 97)

Puffed Bread

— *Phulka* —

225 g/8 oz chappati flour or
wholemeal flour, sifted
¼ teaspoon salt
about 150 ml/¼ pint water

This bread takes about 1 hour to prepare. Place the flour
and salt in a bowl, then gradually mix in the water to
make a sticky dough. Knead the dough for 5 to 7 minutes,
or until it is smooth and elastic, and no longer sticky. For
phulka, the dough must be kneaded with the knuckles,
using firm downward pressure. Place the dough on a
lightly floured plate, cover it and leave it to stand for
30 minutes. If used before it has had a chance to settle, the
dough will be elastic and difficult to roll out.

Divide the dough into six pieces. Dust one piece of
dough with flour, sprinkle flour on the palms of your
hands and roll the dough into a ball. Flatten the ball
between your palms, then roll it into a round measuring
15 cm/6 in. in diameter and about 3 mm/⅛ in thick. Repeat
with the remaining pieces of dough.

Heat a tawa or griddle. Slap the phulka on to the tawa
and cook it until it is half cooked, but not browned. Turn
the bread over. The next stage demands a little practice
but once you've made a couple of phulkas you should
have no problem. Raise the heat and move the tawa or
griddle so that the edge is immediately over the flame or
heat. Push the phulka so that a third of it is over the edge
of the griddle, exposed directly to the heat. Use a pad of
absorbent kitchen paper or a pair of kitchen tongs to
rotate the phulka over the heat; it will puff up as the
cooking process is completed. Serve hot. MAKES 6

Picnic Bread

— *Rogni Roti* —

225 g/8 oz chappati flour or
wholemeal flour, sifted
½ teaspoon salt
4–6 tablespoons milk
50 g/2 oz butter, melted
butter for cooking

This bread takes about 30 minutes to prepare. Sift the flour
and salt into a bowl, make a well in the centre and pour in
the milk. Add the melted butter and – using your fingers
at first, then your knuckles – work the ingredients
together to make a firm dough. Divide the dough into
about six equal portions and shape each piece into a ball,
then flatten the dough between the palms of your hands to
make a disc. Roll out each piece to give a 13-cm/5-in circle
and prick the dough all over with a fork.

Heat a tawa or griddle over a medium heat and grease it
with a little butter. Cook the bread gently pressing it
down slightly until browned on both sides. Spoon a little
melted butter over the bread and serve hot or cold. MAKES
ABOUT 6

Note: Rogni Roti is similar in thickness to a biscuit, but it
is pliable when cooked. This bread keeps quite well, and
it is often packed for snacks to take on journeys. In India,
a packed lunch for travelling might be a hard-boiled egg,
Tomato Chutney (page 106) and Picnic Bread.

Layered Unleavened Bread

Paratha

225 g/8 oz chappati flour or wholemeal flour, sifted
½ teaspoon salt
scant 150 ml/¼ pint water
25 g/1 oz butter, melted
oil for cooking

This bread takes about 1½ hours to prepare. Prepare the dough as for Puffed Bread (opposite page). Knead the dough and leave it to settle for 30 minutes.

Divide the dough into three portions and roll each into a 25-cm/10-in circle. Lightly mark the circles of dough into three sections as shown in diagram 1. Brush the bread with melted butter and sprinkle a little flour over it. Following diagram 2, fold the left hand section over the middle of the circle. Brush the top of the folded dough with melted butter and sprinkle with a little flour, then fold the right hand portion over as shown in diagram 3. Brush the top with melted butter and sprinkle with flour. Mark the dough into three portions, as shown in diagram 4, and fold the dough according to diagrams 5 and 6, brushing each fold with butter and sprinkling with flour. You should end up with a multi-layered piece of dough

roughly in the shape of a small square. Roll out the dough, retaining the square shape as far as possible, to give a paratha which is about 15–20 cm/6–8 in square.

Heat a tawa or griddle over a medium heat and grease it with a little butter. Cook the bread gently pressing it begins to cook. Turn, press the edges again, and pour ½ teaspoon of oil on the tawa round the edges of the bread; the oil seeps under the paratha and this helps the underside to cook. The paratha should be pressed on to the tawa throughout cooking to ensure that it is evenly cooked. Turn once more and again pour ½ teaspoon of oil round the edges of the paratha. The bread is cooked when it is freckled on both sides with small brown patches. Serve hot. MAKES 3

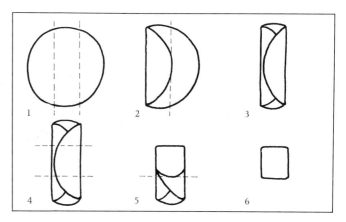

95

Fine Chappati

———— Ulteh Taweh Ki Chappati ————

225 g/8 oz chappati flour or wholemeal flour, sifted
¼ teaspoon salt · generous 150 ml/¼ pint water

This bread takes about 1½ hours to prepare. Sift the flour and salt into a bowl. Mix in the water to make a very soft dough. Knead for 5 to 7 minutes, then leave the dough to rest for 1 hour. Split the dough into three portions and roll them into balls. Flatten each portion to make a small round about the size of the palm of your hand. Sprinkle generously with flour and roll each piece of dough into as large and thin a circle as possible, making sure that the bread is not too large for the griddle.

A tawa is best to cook this bread. If you do not have one, then the bread can be cooked on a large griddle. Turn the tawa upside down over the heat so that the rounded side faces up. Heat the tawa, then use the rolling pin to pick up the chappati. Stretch the edges of the bread and lay it on the hot surface. When the bread begins to darken turn it over and continue cooking until the dough is cooked, turning once more to ensure even cooking. Serve hot. MAKES 3

Note: Ulteh Taweh Ki Chappati is a large thin chappati which dries up quickly, so it should always be kept in a cloth after cooking.

Deep-fried Bread

———— Puri ————

225 g/8 oz chappati flour *or*
wholemeal flour, sifted
½ teaspoon salt
25 g/1 oz butter
scant 150 ml/¼ pint water
oil for deep frying

This bread takes about 1½ hours to prepare. Sift the flour and salt into a bowl, then rub in the butter with your fingers. Add the water and work the ingredients together to make a firm dough. Knead the dough for about 4 minutes, then leave it to rest for 1 hour.

Divide the dough into eight portions and roll each piece into a ball. Flatten the balls into small discs about the size of the palm of your hand, then roll them out to give rounds measuring 10 cm/4 in. in diameter and 3 mm/⅛ in thick.

Heat the oil for deep frying to 185c/370F and deep fry each puri, pouring hot oil over the exposed surface of the bread during cooking to make it puff up. Serve hot. MAKES 8

Fried Pasties

— *Samosas* —

1 quantity Samosa Mince (page 48)
or Zebra Potatoes (page 59)
DOUGH
225 g/8 oz plain flour
pinch of salt
150 ml/¼ pint water
rice flour for dusting
oil for cooking

These snacks take about 1½ hours to prepare. Prepare the mince or potato stuffing following the recipe instructions. Prepare the dough according to the recipe for Two-layered Bread (page 98) using plain flour instead of chappati flour. Use rice flour for dusting the dough and roll out the rotis as finely as possible.

Cook the bread gently on a hot tawa or griddle so that each layer of dough is barely cooked and not browned. Separate the two layers and keep them wrapped in a cloth until required. Cut the rounds into 5-cm/2-in strips (see diagram 1). Neaten each strip so that the ends are triangular and roughly mark the strips into five sections as shown in diagram 2. Place a heaped teaspoon of the chosen filling at one end of the dough between A and B, then fold the dough over and over to make a triangular shaped pasty (diagrams 3 and 4). Continue folding until the strip of dough is used and the filling is sealed in. Tuck the final loose piece of dough neatly between a fold so that the samosa will not come undone during cooking. You may have to trim the end of the dough to make sure that it is small enough to tuck in.

Fry the samosas gently in oil to a depth of 1 cm/½ in, turning once, until they are crisp and golden. Drain on absorbent kitchen paper and serve hot. MAKES ABOUT 18

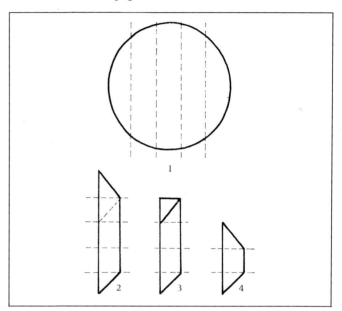

97

Stuffed Fried Bread

―――― *Kheema Puri* ――――

100 g/4 oz plain flour
100 g/4 oz semolina
pinch of salt
40 g/1½ oz butter
150 ml/¼ pint water
oil for deep frying
FILLING
(Sada Kheema)
450 g/1 lb finely ground beef
1½ teaspoons Standard Four Spices (page 12)
1 teaspoon salt
freshly ground black pepper
2 tablespoons oil
6 tablespoons Hara Masala (page 12)
juice of 1 lemon

This bread takes about 1½–1¾ hours to prepare. First prepare the kheema: put the beef, Standard Four Spices, salt and pepper in a saucepan, then cover it and cook gently for 10 to 15 minutes. If the meat is cooked over a medium heat it will not stick, but if necessary add the oil. Uncover the pan, increase the heat and cook, stirring continuously, until the meat is crisp and dark brown. As it cooks, break up the meat with a potato masher. Sprinkle the Hara Masala and lemon juice over the kheema and set aside to cool.

Sift and mix the flour, semolina and salt. Using your fingers, rub the butter into the mixture, then work the water into the dry ingredients to make a dough. Knead for 10 to 15 minutes to break down the granular texture of the semolina. Flatten the mixture several times with a rolling pin as this helps to make a smooth dough. It is important to press firmly in order to break down the semolina. Leave the dough to rest for 20 minutes.

Divide the dough into six portions and roll each into a ball, then flatten these between the palm of your hands and roll out into 10-cm/4-in circles. Place a spoonful of the filling on one circle of dough, dampen the edges and cover with a second circle, pressing the edges together well to seal in the filling. Make 1-cm/½-in cuts all the way round the edges of the puri (see diagram 1) and fold alternate flaps of pastry inwards so that the puri looks like a cogged wheel (diagram 2). Repeat with the remaining dough and filling.

Heat the oil for deep frying to 185c/370F and fry the puri until they are puffed and golden. Serve hot. MAKES 3

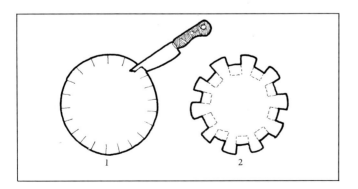

Deep-fried Snacks

―――― *Lukhmi* ――――

(Illustrated on page 23)

100 g/4 oz semolina
100 g/4 oz plain flour, sifted
½ teaspoon salt · 40 g/1½ oz butter
150 ml/¼ pint water
¼ quantity Sada Kheema (opposite)
1 tablespoon Hara Masala (page 12)
juice of ½ lemon · oil for deep frying

This snack takes about 1 hour to prepare. Prepare the dough exactly as for Stuffed Fried Bread (previous recipe), using the semolina, flour, salt, butter and water. Mix the Sada Kheema with the Hara Masala and lemon juice.

Divide the dough in half and roll each portion into a 25–30-cm/10–12-in disc. Using a knife, mark one disc into three strips, first vertically, then horizontally to give nine portions. Place a teaspoonful of the Sada Kheema on each portion, leaving plenty of room between the small mounds of filling. Lightly brush the dough with water between the filling. Cover with the second piece of dough and press firmly between the mounds of filling to seal them in well. Cut between the filled portions to make roughly square shaped Lukhmi. Heat the oil for deep frying to 185c/370F and fry the Lukhmi until golden. Drain on absorbent kitchen paper and serve. MAKES 9

Two-layered Bread

―――― *Do Parad Roti* ――――

(Illustrated on page 33)

225 g/8 oz chappati flour or wholemeal
flour, sifted · ¼ teaspoon salt
150 ml/¼ pint water · 25 g/1 oz butter

This bread takes about 1½ to 1¾ hours to prepare. Sift the flour and salt into a bowl. Add all but 1 tablespoon of the water and mix to make a firm dough. Knead for 5 to 7 minutes, then leave for 1 hour. Knead briefly, then divide the dough into six portions. Shape these into balls and flatten them into discs or *peras*.

Dust the discs with flour and roll them into 13-cm/5-in rounds. Melt the butter and brush a little over one circle of dough. Sprinkle with flour, then lay a second piece of dough on top. Roll the double layer of dough into a 20-cm/8-in circle. Repeat with the remaining dough.

Heat a tawa or griddle. Slap the bread on to the tawa or griddle and press the edges. As soon as it begins to cook, turn it over and cook the other side. Press the edges until the roti puffs. Turn again, pressing and the layers will separate. Take the bread off the tawa separating the two layers, wrap it in a cloth and serve hot. MAKES 6

Subtle Beef Kabaabs (page 54) with Stuffed Fried Bread, Spicy French Beans (page 78), Coriander Chutney (page 106) and chopped tomatoes with onion

White Lentil Fritters

—————— Maash Ke Bhajjyeh ——————

100 g/4 oz urud dal
2 green chillies, chopped
2 tablespoons chopped chives
pinch of baking powder
1 teaspoon salt
oil for deep frying

This dish requires 3 hours' soaking and about 30 minutes' preparation. Wash and soak the urud dal for 3 hours. Drain off all the water, then place the dals in a liquidiser with just enough water to cover and blend to a fine paste. If too many urud dal are put into the liquidiser at one time, the blades tend to jam and they will not grind effectively. Mix the paste with the chillies, chives, baking powder and salt.

Heat the oil for deep frying to 185c/370F. Using a dessertspoon and a teaspoon to tease off the mixture, fry spoonfuls of the paste at a time. At first the paste drops to the bottom of the pan and flattens out, then it rises to the surface. The fritters should be light and they may be hollow. If the paste for the first attempt is too thick, the resulting fritter will be rounded and uncooked in the centre, in which case thin the paste with a little extra water. Use a slotted spoon to turn the fritters and fry them until they are golden brown on both sides. Drain on absorbent kitchen paper and serve hot. SERVES 4

Gram Lentil Fritters

—————— Pyaz Ke Bhajjyeh ——————

100 g/4 oz besan flour · pinch of baking powder
1 large clove garlic, crushed
½ teaspoon ground ginger
½ teaspoon chilli powder
¼ teaspoon turmeric · 1 teaspoon salt
150 ml/¼ pint water
4 medium onions, finely sliced
oil for deep frying

These fritters take about 30 minutes to prepare. Sift the besan flour into a bowl, add the baking powder, garlic, spices and salt, then mix thoroughly. Gradually beat the water into the mixed flour and spices, stirring constantly, until a smooth batter is formed. These proportions should produce a thick pouring batter.

Soak the onions in cold water until they are crisp. Drain off all the water and then mix the slices with the batter.

Heat the oil for deep frying to 185c/370F. Tease off and fry a dessertspoonful of the onion batter mix at a time. Use a slotted spoon to lift out the fritters when they are cooked and golden brown. Drain on absorbent kitchen paper and eat hot. SERVES 6 TO 8

Note: Other vegetables or meats can be made into fritters instead of the onions. The secret is to cut whatever is used into very small pieces or strips so that when the batter is cooked the contents are also cooked. Here are some more suggestions: try fine strips of frying steak, small pieces of breast of chicken, peeled cooked prawns, small nuggets of fish, small florets of cauliflower or broccoli, finely chopped white cabbage, slivers of green pepper or small tender brussels sprouts.

Bouncing Potatoes

Aloo Bonde

4 medium potatoes
1 quantity batter (see Gram Lentil Fritters, opposite)
3 tablespoons Hara Masala (page 12)
juice of 1 lemon
1 teaspoon salt
$\frac{1}{4}$ teaspoon ground black pepper
oil for deep frying

This dish takes about 30 minutes to prepare. Boil, then peel the potatoes. While the potatoes are boiling, make the batter.

Mash the cooked potatoes and mix them with the Hara Masala, lemon juice, salt and pepper. Heat the oil for deep frying to 185c/370F. Shape the potato mixture into round balls the size of a walnut, then dip each one into the batter. The potato mixture should be completely covered in batter otherwise it will disintegrate during cooking. Serve immediately. MAKES 24

Okra Crunch

Tali Bhendi

225 g/8 oz okra
oil for deep frying
$\frac{1}{2}$ teaspoon salt
$\frac{1}{4}$ teaspoon chilli powder

This dish takes about 20 minutes to prepare. Wash the okra, then trim off and discard the ends and cut them into fine rings. Heat the oil for deep frying to 185c/370F. Throw in a handful of okra at a time. Fry until the okra changes colour (it should be lightly browned), remove and drain the vegetables on absorbent kitchen paper.

Once all the okra is cooked sprinkle with salt and chilli powder and serve. SERVES 4

Note: This is served as an accompaniment to a meal in the same way that a pickle or chutney might be served. The small pieces of okra are not mixed with the meal but they are tasted between mouthfuls. Do not overfry the okra, because once it is dark brown it is impossible to tell if the ringlets are overcooked.

Chutneys and pickles

Chutney is derived from the word *chaatna*, which means to taste. Traditionally chutneys were made in small quantities, served in small bowls, and tasted between mouthfuls during a meal. The idea was to stimulate the appetite. Today there is hardly anybody in India who conforms to this tradition and chutneys are eaten in large quantities. They are mixed up with meats and vegetables or sometimes they are even eaten as a relish with breads.

The difference between a chutney and a pickle is quite straightforward. Pickles are made from fruits and vegetables when they come into season and are intended to keep for a year until the next pickle-making season. Mango is one of the most popular and copiously produced pickles, and 500 to 1,000 firm unripe mangoes have first to be sorted and cleaned. The mangoes are sliced, chopped, then salted and left in the sun. The warmth and the salt draws out any moisture or liquid in the mangoes; meanwhile pounds of spices are weighed out and made ready for use – some ground, some left whole. The ingredients are then mixed in large pickling pans and cooked outside; finally when the pickle has cooled, it's stored in large glazed stoneware jars called *martabans*. The layer of oil on the surface of the pickles not only keeps out any moisture but also seals the surface. Each family has its own traditional recipes (closely guarded secrets) but at pickling time sealed jars are sent round to all the neighbours.

Chutneys are made as required and will not really keep for more than two days. The ingredients for chutneys encompass almost any fruit or vegetable in season. Yogurt is frequently used as a base, with herbs and spices added, or ground roasted nuts and seeds can be included at will. Chutneys are often prepared for a specific meal and may be sweet, sour, hot, mild or even bland – whichever flavour complements the food. They are served in small bowls, but are generally so popular that large quantities have to be made.

Clockwise from top left: Green Chilli Pickle, Chilli and Onion Chutney and Coconut Chutney (all recipes overleaf)

Coconut Chutney

Khopreh Ki Chutney

$\frac{1}{4}$ fresh coconut, grated
1 medium onion, finely chopped
2 dried red chillies, cut into fine slivers
$\frac{1}{4}$ teaspoon chopped fresh root ginger
juice of 1 lemon

This chutney takes about 15 minutes to prepare. Mix all the prepared ingredients with the lemon juice. Serve the chutney in a small bowl. SERVES 4

Chilli and Onion Chutney

Lache Dar Piaz

2 medium onions
3 tablespoons lemon juice
$\frac{1}{2}$ teaspoon salt
pinch of freshly ground black pepper
$\frac{1}{2}$ teaspoon chilli powder

This chutney takes about 10 minutes to prepare. Slice the onions extremely thinly, then separate the slices into rings. Wash the onions in cold water to make them crisp and remove some of their excess power. Drain thoroughly and mix with all the other ingredients. Serve lightly chilled. SERVES 4

Note: If the chutney is left to stand for a long time the salt draws out the liquid from the onions; this should be drained off before serving.

Green Chilli Pickle

Hari Mirchi Ka Achaar

150 ml/$\frac{1}{4}$ pint oil
1 teaspoon cumin seeds
10 curry leaves
150 ml/$\frac{1}{4}$ pint fresh lemon juice
4 cloves garlic, crushed
1 tablespoon ground cumin
1 tablespoon ground coriander
1 teaspoon ground mustard seeds
$\frac{1}{4}$ teaspoon ground fenugreek
$\frac{1}{4}$ teaspoon ground kalonji
12 medium green chillies, slit lengthways
1 tablespoon sea salt

This chutney takes about 15 minutes to prepare. Heat the oil in a saucepan; when hot add the cumin seeds and curry leaves. Cover the pan and remove it from the heat, then allow to cool for 2 to 3 minutes.

Add the lemon juice, garlic, all the ground spices, chillies and salt, then replace the pan on the heat. Cook gently over a medium heat for 5 minutes. Cool without covering the pan.

To store the chutney, pot it while still warm and keep it in the refrigerator for a few weeks. SERVES 10 TO 12

Garlic Pickle

— Lehsun Ka Achaar —

3 whole bulbs fresh garlic
3 tablespoons sea salt · 8 green chillies, ground
150 ml/¼ pint bottled, unsweetened lemon juice
150 ml/¼ pint oil · ½ teaspoon mustard seeds
½ teaspoon fenugreek seeds
1 teaspoon cumin seeds
¼ teaspoon kalonji · 6 curry leaves

This pickle takes about 45 minutes to prepare. Peel all the cloves of garlic and mix them with the sea salt, then set aside. Blend the green chillies in a liquidiser with the lemon juice.

Heat the oil in a saucepan and add the mustard seeds, fenugreek and cumin seeds with the kalonji and curry leaves. Cover the pan and remove it from the heat, then set aside for 2 to 3 minutes. Return the pan to the heat and add the garlic, then cook gently for 5 minutes. Pour in the lemon juice mixture and simmer gently, uncovered, until the oil rises to the surface – about 10 to 15 minutes.

Spoon the pickle into warmed jars and cover with airtight lids, then leave to stand for 3 days before eating. This allows time for the lemon juice to work its way into the garlic. Store for up to 2 weeks in the refrigerator. SERVES 10 TO 12

Mint Chutney

— Pudina Ki Chutney —

2 tablespoons desiccated coconut
3 tablespoons lemon juice
2 or 3 whole green chillies, chopped
1 large bunch fresh mint, chopped
1½ teaspoons salt
pinch of freshly ground black pepper
1 teaspoon sugar

This chutney takes about 10 minutes to prepare. Roast and grind the desiccated coconut. Mix with all the other ingredients and blend in the liquidiser to a creamy consistency. Serve lightly chilled. SERVES 4 TO 6

Tomato Chutney

—— Tomate Ki Chutney ——

1 medium onion, finely chopped
25 g/1 oz Hara Masala (page 12)
3 tablespoons fresh lemon juice
1½ teaspoons salt
pinch of ground black pepper
4 medium tomatoes (firm ones which are
not quite ripe)

This chutney takes about 15 minutes to prepare. Mix all the ingredients apart from the tomatoes and put them in the refrigerator to chill. Finely chop the tomatoes and add them to the mixture just before serving. If the tomatoes are added too soon the chutney becomes watery as they give up their juice. Serve garnished with mint. SERVES 4

Note: The secret of success for this chutney is to ensure that all the ingredients are finely chopped to the same size.

Sesame Chutney

—— Til Ki Chutney ——

4 tablespoons sesame seeds
150 ml/¼ pint tamarind extract (page 16)
2 teaspoons salt
2 tablespoons chopped fresh coriander leaves
3 green chillies
generous pinch of black pepper

This chutney takes about 15 minutes to prepare. Roast the sesame seeds until lightly browned, then cool and grind them finely in a coffee grinder. Place the sesame seeds with all the remaining ingredients in a liquidiser and blend them together to make a smooth paste. Serve in a small bowl. SERVES 4

Gooseberry Chutney

—— Leori Ki Chutney ——

225 g/8 oz unripened gooseberries
½ medium onion, finely chopped
1 small green pepper, deseeded and finely chopped
1 green chilli, finely chopped
2 tablespoons chopped fresh coriander leaves
1 teaspoon honey
½ teaspoon ground black pepper
2 teaspoons salt

This chutney takes about 15 minutes to prepare. Top, tail and quarter the gooseberries, then mix them with all the other ingredients and serve chilled. SERVES 6

Coriander Chutney

—— Kothmir Ki Chutney ——

50 g/2 oz chopped fresh coriander leaves
2 or 3 green chillies
½ medium onion, roughly chopped
4 tablespoons lemon juice
2 teaspoons salt
pinch of ground black pepper

This chutney takes only a few minutes to prepare. Blend all the ingredients together in a liquidiser, then chill the chutney before serving. SERVES 4

Lime or Lemon Pickle

Nimboo Ka Achaar

6 fresh limes *or* 5 lemons with their skins
6 tablespoons sea salt
16 cloves garlic
300 ml/½ pint fresh lemon juice
6 green chillies
4 tablespoons ground cumin
4 tablespoons chilli powder
600 ml/1 pint water

This pickle takes about 1 hour to prepare. Wash the limes or lemons, then place them in a saucepan with 3 tablespoons of the salt. Pour in enough water to cover the fruit and bring to the boil, then turn off the heat and leave the fruit to soak for 10 minutes, or until the skins are tender. If the lemon skins burst the pickle will not keep.

Drain the fruit, dry it on absorbent kitchen paper and leave to cool. Cut the cold fruit into eighths. Sprinkle the remaining salt over the fruit, then mix in half the garlic cloves and all the remaining ingredients. Crush the rest of the garlic and add it to the pickle. Bottle and keep for 3 to 4 days before eating. Store in an airtight jar in the refrigerator. SERVES 12 TO 15

Gooseberry Pickle

Gooseberry Ka Achaar

225 g/8 oz firm young gooseberries
2 tablespoons sea salt
2 tablespoons ground cumin
4 large cloves garlic, crushed
1 tablespoon chilli powder
150 ml/¼ pint oil
½ teaspoon fenugreek seeds
8 curry leaves
2 tablespoons vinegar
1 teaspoon sugar

This pickle takes about 1 to 2 hours to soak and about 30 minutes to prepare. Wash and thoroughly dry the gooseberries, then top and tail them and place them in a bowl with the salt. This will draw out the excess moisture from the fruit.

Roast the ground cumin in a heavy-based saucepan until it's a shade darker than it was when you started. Do not overcook the spice or it will become bitter. Mix the cumin with the garlic and chilli powder and set aside. The moisture in the garlic brings out the flavour in the spices.

Heat the oil in a heavy-based saucepan, then remove the pan from the heat and add the fenugreek seeds and curry leaves. Cover and leave to cool for 2 to 3 minutes. Add the garlic mixture, then return the pan to the heat and fry for 5 minutes, or until the garlic smell has died down. Take care not to overfry the mixture or the chilli may burn.

Drain the gooseberries and add them to the spices then leave over a low heat for 5 minutes or until the oil surfaces. Pour in the vinegar and stir in the sugar, then leave to cool. Store in airtight jars. SERVES 12 TO 15

Mango Pickle

Chote Tukron Ka Achaar

3 teaspoons mustard seeds
2 unripened mangoes or medium cooking apples
(hard and sour ones)
150 ml/¼ pint oil
10 curry leaves
½ teaspoon fenugreek seeds
3 teaspoons ground ginger
6 large cloves garlic, crushed
8 teaspoons chilli powder
½ teaspoon turmeric
6 teaspoons ground cumin
150 ml/¼ pint vinegar
1 teaspoon sugar
1 tablespoon salt

This pickle takes about 40 minutes to prepare. Briefly grind the mustard seeds in a coffee grinder. Peel the mangoes and chop them or the apples into 1-cm/½-in cubes (do not peel the apples). Heat the oil in a heavy-based saucepan, then add the curry leaves and fenugreek and remove the pan from the heat. Cover and leave to cool for 2 to 3 minutes.

Return the pan to the heat and add the ginger, garlic, chilli powder, turmeric, cumin and half the ground mustard seeds. Stir over a medium heat for 2 to 3 minutes. Add the diced mangoes or apples with any juice and continue cooking, uncovered, stirring constantly until the oil surfaces – about 5 minutes. Do not cover the pan while cooking.

At the end of this time the apples should still be firm but not too hard. Just before turning off the heat, pour in the vinegar and add the remaining mustard seeds, sugar and salt. Cool; bottle in airtight jars. SERVES ABOUT 15

Mixed Vegetable Pickle

Miloni Tarkari Kar Achaar

300 ml/½ pint oil *plus* oil for deep frying
2 tablespoons shelled broad beans
2 tablespoons diced French beans
2 tablespoons shelled peas
100 g/4 oz small pickling onions
1 teaspoon salt
2 tablespoons cumin seeds
1 teaspoon fenugreek seeds
12 curry leaves
6 large cloves garlic, crushed
3 tablespoons chilli powder
300 ml/½ pint tomato purée (made from 1 kg/2 lb
fresh tomatoes)
150 ml/¼ pint vinegar
2 teaspoons sugar

This pickle takes about 30 to 40 minutes to prepare. Heat the oil for deep frying to 185c/370f and lightly fry all the vegetables, then drain them on absorbent kitchen paper. Sprinkle with a little of the salt. Heat the measured oil in a heavy-based saucepan. Add the cumin seeds, fenugreek seeds and curry leaves. Cover the pan and remove it from the heat. After 2 or 3 minutes add the garlic and chilli powder, then return the pan to the heat and stir for 1 to 2 minutes, taking care not to burn the chilli powder. Now add the tomato purée, remaining salt and vegetables and continue cooking for a further 5 to 7 minutes. Just before turning off the heat, pour in the vinegar and stir in the sugar, then allow the pickle to cool without covering the pan. Spoon into sterilised pots and cover tightly.

The pickle should be bright red, covered with a thick layer of oil on top. After two or three days the vinegar and spices will have impregnated the vegetables and the pickle will be ready to eat. SERVES ABOUT 15

Desserts and sherbets

A number of Indian desserts, notably halvas, require hours of patient stirring and fiddly decoration. On formal occasions, when at least five desserts are served, the time-consuming halvas covered with silver and gold foil are an absolute necessity. The elaborate filigree decoration reflects not only the cook's talents but also her culture. At a formal wedding, whispered comments criticise the cook's breeding through the presentation of her desserts. A successful display will crown the day's achievements.

Dessert cookery in India has its traditions. For example, carrots are used for their sweetness, while beetroot is used for its intense colour. One style of dessert cookery is to prepare the sweet in layers. For example, a disc of halva is prepared then covered with either gold or silver leaf. Then another disc of halva, cut into elaborate geometrical designs, is laid on top. The varaq gleams through giving a delightful lattice work effect.

Sherbets are not normally drunk at meals and water is the most common drink to accompany a spicy meal. However, there are a few sherbet recipes in this chapter and you may like to serve them to complete your Indian feast.

Yogurt Drink, Lime Cooler and Milk Rose Dessert
(all recipes overleaf)

Milk Rose Dessert

— Kheer —

100 g/4 oz basmati rice
100 g/4 oz blanched almonds
2.25 litres/4 pints full cream milk
2 cardamoms
225 g/8 oz sugar

DECORATION (OPTIONAL)
1 pink rose
silver varaq
blanched almonds, cut into flakes
blanched pistachio nuts, cut into flakes

This dish needs 3 hours' soaking time and about 2 hours to prepare. Soak the rice in cold water for 3 hours. At the end of the soaking time, drain off the water and spread the rice on absorbent kitchen paper to dry. Once the rice has dried finely grind it in a coffee grinder or liquidiser. Press the ground rice through a fine sieve.

Soak the blanched almonds in cold water for 30 minutes. Blend the almonds with a quarter of the milk to make a fine purée.

Bring the milk to the boil in a large non-stick or heavy-based saucepan. Keep an eagle eye on the milk as it simmers to prevent it from boiling over. Continue cooking gently, stirring occasionally, until the milk has reduced by half. Add the ground rice and continue cooking. If any solids cling to the side of the pan, then use a wooden spoon to stir them into the milk. Continue simmering until the milk is further reduced by half.

Crush the cardamoms, then add them with the sugar to the milk and continue simmering for 5 minutes. Remove the pan from the heat and allow to cool. Stir from time to time during cooling so that any skin that forms is well mixed into the kheer. Transfer to a suitable serving dish and chill.

The kheer can be eaten just the way it is, but on special occasions in India additional decoration would be lavished on the dessert: the kheer would be poured into individual bowls or dishes, then decorated with varaq, almond and pistachio flakes, and some more rose petals. SERVES 6 TO 8

Lime Cooler

— Nimboo Ka Sherbet —

4 fresh limes
1.15 litres/2 pints water
4 tablespoons sugar
lime slices to decorate

This drink takes 10 minutes to prepare. Squeeze all the juice from the limes and mix it with the water and sugar. Chill thoroughly. Serve the sherbet in a glass jug, or in individual glasses, with plenty of ice. Float lime slices in each glass. SERVES 4

Yogurt Drink

— Lussi —

600 ml/1 pint natural yogurt
600 ml/1 pint water, chilled
6 teaspoons sugar (or to taste)
1 tablespoon keora essence
salt

This drink takes about 10 minutes to prepare. Place all the ingredients in a liquidiser with a pinch of salt and blend together, then pour the drink into glasses and add a few ice cubes to each. SERVES 4 TO 6

Baked Egg and Saffron Halva

—————— *Andon Ki Peosi* ——————

¼ teaspoon saffron strands
3 tablespoons boiling water
100 g/4 oz blanched almonds
450 ml/¾ pint milk · 350 g/12 oz sugar
6 eggs · 225 g/8 oz unsalted butter, melted
3 tablespoons dried whole milk

This dish takes about 1¼ hours to prepare. Pound the saffron and mix it with the boiling water. Soak the almonds in cold water. Heat 300 ml/½ pint of the milk and the sugar in a pan until the sugar dissolves. Cool. Set a few almonds aside for the decoration. Blend the remaining nuts and milk together to form a smooth paste.

Now, mix the eggs, sweetened milk, butter, dried milk, almond paste and 2 tablespoons of the saffron liquid. Pour this mixture into a greased 18 × 26-cm/7 × 10½-in tin to a depth of no more than 1.5 cm/¾ in. Cut the reserved almonds into fine slivers and scatter these over the mixture. Sprinkle the saffron water over the entire surface of the halva and bake in a moderate oven (180C, 350F, gas 4) for 45 minutes, until the surface is golden brown.

Cool the halva in the tin, then cut it into diamond shapes before serving. SERVES 12 TO 16

Carrot Halva

—————— *Gajar Ka Halva* ——————

¼ teaspoon saffron strands
4 tablespoons boiling water · 900 ml/1½ pints milk
100 g/4 oz unsalted butter · 1 teaspoon oil
450 g/1 lb fresh juicy carrots, finely grated
2 cloves · 3 cardamoms, crushed
175 g/6 oz sugar · 1 tablespoon rose water
10 blanched almonds or pistachio nuts, cut into
fine slivers · sliver varak (optional)

This halva takes about 1½ hours to prepare. Pound the saffron and mix it with the boiling water. Bring the milk to the boil and simmer until it is reduced by a third, taking care that it does not boil over or burn.

Melt the butter with the oil in a saucepan. Add the carrots, cloves and crushed cardamoms. Fry gently until the carrots turn a dark orange – about 15 minutes. Strain the milk on to the carrots and simmer gently, stirring occasionally, until it completely evaporates. Add the sugar and continue to cook, stirring constantly over a low heat, until the sugar melts and the mixture no longer clings to the side of the pan.

Remove the pan from the heat. Pour in the rose water and saffron, cover and leave to cool. While still warm, pour the halva on to a flat serving platter and leave to set. Cover with the almonds or pistachio nuts and lay varak (if used) on top before serving. SERVES 4 TO 6

Stewed Indian Apricots

———— Qhoobani Ka Meetha ————

350 g/12 oz qhoobani · 225 g/8 oz sugar
sliver varaq for decoration (optional)

*This dish requires overnight soaking and about 1¼ hours'
preparation.* Wash the qhoobani in frequent changes of
cold water until the water runs clear. Soak the fruit in
enough cold water to cover it by 5 cm/2 in. Allow at least
12 hours for the dried fruit to soften and swell.

With a sharp knife slit the sides of the apricots, then
carefully remove and reserve the stones without unduly
damaging the fruit. Put the qhoobani and the liquid in
which they were soaked in a saucepan. Rinse the stones in
300 ml/½ pint water and add this liquid to the pan. Bring
just to the boil, then simmer very gently for 15 minutes.
Add the sugar and continue to simmer for a further
30 minutes. If you must stir the qhoobani do not break up
the fruit. Transfer to a serving bowl and cool.

While the fruit is cooking remove the seeds from the
stones. Do this by cracking the stones in a nut cracker or
by wrapping them in kitchen paper and breaking them in
a large pestle and mortar. Blanch the seeds in boiling water
and rub off their skins. Decorate the qhoobani with the
almond seeds and sliver varaq (if used) then serve with
whipped cream. SERVES 8 TO 10

Note: Qhoobani are a variety of apricot indigenous to
India and they are much smaller than the apricots
commonly sold in Europe. Dried they are sold by most
Indian grocers and in some health food or whole food
shops. It is worth buying several packets when you have
the opportunity, as they can be stored for some time in a
cool place.

Ramadan Dessert

———— Sheer Khorma ————

4 almonds · 4 pistachio nuts
1 tablespoon raisins
1 tablespoon chirongi nuts
1.75 litres/3 pints milk
100 g/4 oz sevian or vermicelli,
broken into small pieces
2 cloves · 2 cardamoms
40 g/1½ oz unsalted butter · 100 g/4 oz sugar

*This dessert requires 1½ to 2 hours' soaking time and about 2
hours' preparation.* Blanch the almonds and pistachio nuts
in boiling water for a few minutes then drain them and rub
off their skins. Soak the blanched nuts, raisins and
chirongi nuts separately in cold water for 1 to 2 hours. Cut
the almonds and pistachio nuts into fine slivers.

Bring the milk to the boil, reduce the heat and simmer
gently, stirring occasionally. While the milk is simmering
fry the sevian or vermicelli, cloves and cardamoms in
25 g/1 oz of the butter until the sevian is light golden, then
add the fried ingredients to the milk. Continue simmering.

Fry the raisins and chirongi nuts in the remaining
butter until they are pale golden. The raisins should be
well swollen. Add the sugar to the milk and continue
simmering until the milk has reduced to half its original
quantity. Add the fried chirongi nuts and raisins and
serve hot, decorated with the almonds and pistachios.
SERVES 8

Note: Sheer Khorma is traditionally prepared at the end of
the Ramadan fast on the day of Id. Visits are paid to
friends and neighbours and each person who enters the
house must taste the Sheer Khorma. The major ingredient
is sevian: this is an extremely fine pasta made from wheat
flour. The finest variety should be used. Available from
most Indian grocers, the long strands (like vermicelli) are
broken into very small pieces before cooking.

Saffron and Almond Spongy Dessert

———— *Double Roti Ka Meetha* ————

$\frac{1}{4}$ teaspoon saffron strands
4 tablespoons boiling water
oil for cooking · knob of butter
4 medium slices white bread, with crusts removed
300 ml/$\frac{1}{2}$ pint milk
5 tablespoons ground almonds
100 g/4 oz sugar
50 g/2 oz dried whole milk
1 tablespoon rose water
5 or 6 pistachio nuts, finely chopped
silver varaq to decorate (optional)

This dish takes about 1 hour to prepare. Pound the saffron and mix it with the boiling water. Heat a little oil with a knob of butter, then fry each slice of bread on both sides until golden. Drain the bread on absorbent kitchen paper, then cut each slice in half diagonally. Grease a large, flat ovenproof dish or baking tin and lay the bread slices close together on it, but not overlapping.

Heat the milk in a saucepan with the ground almonds and add the sugar, then heat gently, stirring continuously until all the sugar has dissolved. Remove the pan from the heat and stir in the dried milk powder. The milk will become creamy. Mix 1 tablespoon of the saffron liquid into the milk. Pour this mixture over the bread, allowing it to soak in, then sprinkle the rest of the saffron water and the rose water on top. Scatter the pistachio nuts over and bake in a moderate oven (180C, 350F, gas 4) for 30 minutes, or until the milk is absorbed.

Cool slightly, then lift the slices on to a serving dish. Cover with varaq (if used) and serve cold with fresh cream. SERVES 4 TO 6

Almond Halva

———— *Badaam Ke Laoz* ————

225 g/8 oz shelled almonds
about 450 g/1 lb sugar

This dessert requires 3 hours' soaking time and takes about 45 minutes to prepare. Soak the almonds in boiling water. Replace the water with fresh boiling water after 10 minutes. Leave for a few minutes, then drain the nuts and rub off their skins. Soak the blanched almonds in cold water for 1 to 2 hours. The almonds will become soft and tender.

Blend the almonds with a little water in a liquidiser to make a smooth paste. Do this in batches so as not to strain the liquidiser. Pour the almond purée into a very large heavy-based or non-stick saucepan and cook over a medium heat, stirring constantly, until most of the water has evaporated. Remove from the heat and push the purée to one side of the pan. The mixture should be fairly dry and very thick. Add the sugar to the pan – the quantity should be roughly equal in volume to the almond mixture. A visual estimate is quite adequate.

Return the pan to the heat, mix the ingredients and cook over a low heat until the sugar has dissolved with the almonds. Continue cooking, at first the liquid purée is easy to handle but gradually, as it cooks, the water evaporates and the purée thickens, bubbles and spits. Keep the heat low so that the mixture does not spit too much. Continue cooking, stirring continuously, until the mixture thickens and leaves the sides of the pan.

Remove the pan from the heat and leave for 15 to 20 minutes. When ready, the halva should be firm and dry to the touch. Pour the halva into a buttered Swiss roll tin, spreading it out to a depth of 1 cm/$\frac{1}{2}$ in. Flatten the surface with a palette knife dampened in hot water, leave until half set then cut into small diamonds and allow these to harden before serving. MAKES ABOUT 40 PIECES

Honeydew Melon Ice Cream

———— Khurboozeh Ki Ice Cream ————

2 small honeydew melons
1 (410-g/14.5-oz) can evaporated milk, chilled
4 tablespoons caster sugar
1 teaspoon vanilla essence
300 ml/½ pint double cream

This dish takes about 1 hour to prepare and it requires several hours' freezing. Wash and quarter the melons. Remove their seeds, then scoop out all the flesh in small pieces. Blend the melon with the sugar, vanilla essence and evaporated milk in a liquidiser until smooth and light. Pour into a freezer container and freeze until half frozen.

When the melon mixture is beginning to solidify, lightly whip the cream. Whisk the ice cream thoroughly to break up all the ice crystals, then whisk the ice cream once more when it is half frozen. Freeze until firm.

Transfer the container to the refrigerator 30 minutes before serving the ice cream. SERVES 6

Mango Ice Cream

———— Aam Ki Ice Cream ————

1 (410-g/14½-oz) can mangoes
1 (410-g/14.5-oz) can evaporated milk, chilled
4 tablespoons caster sugar

This ice cream takes about 1 hour to prepare and several hours to freeze. Place all the ingredients in a liquidiser and blend together until smooth and light. Pour the mixture into a freezer container and freeze until half frozen. When the ice cream is beginning to solidify whisk it thoroughly, then return it to the freezer until firm.

Transfer the ice cream to the refrigerator about 15 minutes before you intend serving it. SERVES 4 TO 6

Almond Ice Cream

Kulfi

225 g/8 oz blanched almonds
1.75 litres/3 pints milk
225 g/8 oz caster sugar
300 ml/½ pint double cream
2 tablespoons rose water

This ice cream takes about 1 hour to prepare and it requires several hours' freezing. Place the almonds in a basin, cover with cold water and set aside. Reserve 300 ml/½ pint of the milk and bring the rest to the boil in a large heavy-based or non-stick saucepan. Simmer until the milk is reduced by half, stirring from time to time to ensure that any skin or solids that cling to the side of the pan we well mixed with the milk.

Drain the almonds and place three-quarters of them in a liquidiser with the reserved milk. Blend the mixture until the almnds are roughly ground; the mixture should be crunchy. Add the almond mixture and sugar to the hot milk and continue simmering for a further 10 to 20 minutes, stirring constantly. This allows the flavour of the almonds to penetrate the milk. Remove the pan from the heat and allow to cool to room temperature, then place in the refrigerator until well chilled.

Roughly chop the remaining almonds and stir them into the chilled milk with the double cream and rose water. Stir thoroughly so that the ingredients are well and truly mixed. Pour into a metal cone-shaped container, or any other suitable freezer container, and freeze until solid. Transfer to the refrigerator 20 minutes before serving, then turn out if necessary. SERVES 8

Pistachio Ice Cream

Pisteh Ki Ice Cream

225 g/8 oz unsalted shelled pistachio nuts
1.75 litres/3 pints milk · 350 g/12 oz caster sugar

This ice cream takes about 1 hour to prepare and several hours to freeze. Blanch the Pistachios in boiling water for a few minutes, then rub off their skins. Soak the nuts in cold water for 1 hour, then drain them. Set aside 1 tablespoon of the pistachios – cut these into fine slivers and dry them on absorbent kitchen paper.

Pour the milk into a heavy-based or non-stick saucepan and brirg to the boil. Continue simmering until it is reduced to a third – about 600 ml/1 pint. Blend the pistachios with a little water to make a gritty paste, then mix this paste with the sugar in a small heavy-based or non-stick saucepan. Cook until the mixture bubbles – about 15 minutes. It should form a thick paste.

Add half the paste to the milk and mix thoroughly. Pour half the pistachio flavoured milk into an oblong plastic container and freeze. Set the remaining milk and paste aside. As soon as the mixture is firm, remove the container from the freezer and spread the reserved pistachio paste on top. Pour in the rest of the milk mixture and freeze until hard. Remove from the freezer about 15 minutes before serving and leave in the refrigerator. To serve, turn out and slice the ice cream to show the layers. SERVES 6

Mint Sherbert

Sikanjibeen

300 ml/½ pint water
1 kg/2 lb sugar
300 ml/½ pint cider vinegar or white wine vinegar
1 bunch fresh mint

This dish takes about 30 minutes to prepare. Heat the water and just before it boils add the sugar. Stir until the sugar dissolves, then add the vinegar and mint. Now bring the mixture to the boil and simmer for a few minutes. Remove from the heat; cool, strain and bottle.

Dilute a little of the sikanjibeen with water and serve with plenty of ice. MAKES ABOUT 1 LITRE/1¾ PINTS

Tangy Mango Drink

Kairi Ka Sherbet

4 large unripe mangoes
1.15 litres/2 pints water
sugar
crushed ice

This drink takes about 40 minutes to prepare. The first stage is to make the green mangoes tender. They can either be boiled in plenty of water, or they can be covered with hot ashes from a wood fire. The flavour of the mangoes is improved by the fragrance from the wood smoke.

Once the mangoes are tender, squeeze them gently to further soften the inner pulp. The pulp may escape at the join between the stalk and the fruit, so place your thumb over this soft spot as you squeeze the flesh. Once the pulp is soft, remove the stalk. Gently squeeze the mango and collect any juice which is released. Peel off the skin and squeeze any juice from it.

Remove all the pulp from the stone and mix it with the juice. Liquidise the pulp with the water and sugar to taste. Serve with plenty of crushed ice. SERVES 4 TO 6

Watermelon Sherbet

—— Turbooz Ka Sherbet ——

½ small watermelon
sugar

This sherbet takes about 20 minutes to prepare. Wash and dry the melon. Cut it into quarters, then cut the flesh into chunks and remove all the seeds – this is tedious but necessary.

Place the melon and sugar to taste in a liquidiser and blend until smooth. The sugar deepens the natural colour of the melon. Pass the sherbet through a fine sieve, then chill it and serve on ice. SERVES 4 TO 6

Creme de Menthe Drink

—— Pudineh Ka Sherbet ——

12 tablespoons creme de menthe
crushed ice
sparkling spring water
1 lime, finely sliced
mint sprigs

This drink takes about 5 minutes to prepare. Place 3 tablespoons creme de menthe in each of four tall glasses. Add plenty of crushed ice and top up with spring water. Add one or more lime slices to each glass and serve decorated with mint. SERVES 4

Mango Sherbet

———— Aam Ka Rus ————

4 ripe mangoes
sugar to taste
900 ml/1½ pints creamy milk, chilled
crushed ice

This dish takes about 20 minutes to prepare. Squeeze the ripe mangoes to reduce the flesh to a pulp. Hold your fingers over the join between the stalk and fruit to prevent any of the flesh from escaping. Peel the mango and squeeze all the juice from the skin. Remove all the pulpy mango flesh from the stone and mix it with the juice from the skin.

Stir the sugar into the mango and briskly add the cold milk, stirring continuously. Do not use warm milk as it may curdle. Serve in glasses or bowls with plenty of crushed ice. SERVES 4

Rich Almond Sherbet

———— Doodh Ka Sherbet ————

8 pistachio nuts
100 g/4 oz blanched almonds
750 ml/1¼ pints milk
8 teaspoons sugar
2 tablespoons rose water

This sherbet requires 2 hours' soaking and takes about 1 hour to prepare. Blanch the pistachio nuts, remove their skins, then place them in a basin with the almonds and cover with water. Leave to soak for 2 hours or until the nuts are soft. Cut into fine slivers.

Heat the milk with half the almonds and simmer until slightly reduced in volume, stirring the milk occasionally to ensure it does not boil over. Off the heat, add the sugar and continue stirring until the milk is completely cold. This is to prevent a skin from forming.

When cold, add the rest of the almonds and rose water and mix thoroughly. Serve in small glasses with ice cubes and decorated with the pistachio slivers. SERVES 4 TO 6

Note: This creamy, almond flavoured drink is quite exotic and it is usually reserved for special occasions. It is quite rich and should be served in small glasses.

Menu suggestions

The following menu suggestions offer four or five savoury dishes which are ideal for the family or friends. Other dishes can obviously be added according to taste, or if you are catering for a larger group. Desserts are not included as their selection does not affect the choice of the savoury dishes. The dessert you serve depends on taste and the time available. Kulfi and some of the ice creams are an excellent standby because they can be made in batches, frozen and served when needed.

VEGETARIAN MENUS

1

Yellow Lentil Rice
Kichri

Tamarind Eggs
Khatte Ande

Zebra Potatoes
Baghareh Aloo

Sesame Chutney
Til Ki Chutney

2

Vegetable Pilaff
Tarkari Pulao

Mung Beans
Mung Ki Dal

Potato Aureoles
Aloo Tomate

Red Cabbage Salad
Lal Gobi

3

Coriander Rice
Hare Chaval

Okra in Yogurt Sauce
Bhendi Ka Khorma

Tiger Chick Peas
Chole

Spinach Dal
Palak Dal

NON-VEGETARIAN MENUS

1

Puffed Bread
Phulka

Ginger Kabaab
Sulaimani Kabaab

Piquant Tomato Lamb
Tomato Ka Do Pyaza

Weekday Dal
Mithi Dal

2

Plain Rice
Khushka

Garam Masala Mince
Muglai Kheema

Renu's Favourite
Dahi Ki Kari

Crab-stuffed Aubergines
Baigan Khekra

3

Plain Rice
Khushka

Spiced Fried Kidneys
Taleh Hueh Gurdeh

Fenugreek Mince
Kheema Methi

Tomato and Coriander Sauce
Tomate Ki Kari

Index